A HISTORY
OF THE WORLD
IN NUMBERS

A HISTORY OF THE WORLD IN NUMBERS

EMMA MARRIOTT

Michael O'Mara Books Limited

First published in Great Britain in 2014 by
Michael O'Mara Books Limited
9 Lion Yard
Tremadoc Road
London SW4 7NQ

A CIP catalogue record for this book is available from the British Library.

Papers used by Michael O'Mara Books Limited are natural, recyclable products
made from wood grown in sustainable forests. The manufacturing processes
conform to the environmental regulations of the country of origin.

ISBN: 978-1-78243-217-3 in hardback print format
ISBN: 978-1-78243-272-2 in e-book format

1 2 3 4 5 6 7 8 9 10

Jacket illustration and design by Patrick Knowles

Printed and bound by CPI Group (UK) Ltd, Croydon, CR0 4YY

www.mombooks.com

To those who have lived and died before us –
approximately 107.6 billion people

ACKNOWLEDGEMENTS

My thanks go to Louise Dixon, Gabriella Nemeth, Steve Cox and Rod Green for their invaluable help and hard work. I would also like to thank my husband Robin for his sterling support on the home front.

INTRODUCTION

Numbers can reveal much about the history of the world. Their scale or precision can illuminate the sometimes murky and complex history of man, and encapsulate in an instant the enormity or inconsequentiality of an event in the past.

There is also something solid and indisputable about numbers, making them a useful tool for anyone hoping to convey the history of the world in one short book. That's not to say that numbers can't be exaggerated, massaged, or even blatantly wrong – as so often they are – and just like words, they too can distort our view of history.

With this in mind, however, numbers do help to provide a sort of filing system for the past. We love to compartmentalize history, reordering it into tidy folders, labelling them with numbers of note. By this means numbers seem to leap out of the annals of history right into our collective consciousness, to remain lodged in our minds long after other facts have fallen away. The Seven Wonders of the Ancient World, Martin Luther's ninety-five theses, Henry VIII's six wives, Marx's six stages of history, all provide testament to the staying power of numbers.

Different types of numbers can alter our perspective on history. Vast numbers inform us how many people are living on the planet or how many millions are massacred in war. (Too often numbers convey the grim realities of life in the past – how millions have perished from disease, on the battlefield, or merely through the whims of a single deluded monarch or leader.) Large numbers can illustrate the broad sweep of history, from mass movements of populations to the expansion of empires (and often their sudden demise), the profound effects of industrialization and the growth of a global economy.

Smaller numbers, however, are no less significant: they measure the living details of history, the tiny shifts that may have vast consequences. The perfect proportions of Leonardo da Vinci's *Vitruvian Man*, the components of a 'piece of eight' silver coin, the US constitution's thirteenth amendment, all were to have a lasting impact on the history of the world.

The nature of our past – peculiar, extraordinary, often fortuitous – can also be wonderfully illustrated by numbers, from the 12,000 molluscs that it took the Phoenicians to make just 1.5 grams of Tyrian purple, to the $15 million paid by the US government for a vast tract of land known as Louisiana. Mythical (or at least partly mythical) stories of the past, such as the Twelve Knights of the Round Table or the Seven Hills of Rome, can also be given validity or symbolic importance by their association with a number (the numbers seven and twelve are recurring favourites).

Armed with numbers, we can also zoom back and forth through time to compare events and achievements, taking in along the way the massive fifteenth-century fleets of the Chinese Admiral Zheng He (whose size wasn't rivalled in the West until the First World War) to statistics showing that by the 1930s one in five Americans owned a car (a number that the UK didn't reach until the 1960s). We can focus for an instant upon those who actually dealt with numbers – the astronomers, philosophers, engineers, physicists, many of whom exerted and still exert a far-reaching influence on our history, from the Indian scholar Aryabhata, who came up with the invaluable concept of zero, to the British mathematicians of the Second World War who cracked the Enigma system, thereby changing the outcome of a global war.

The History of the World in Numbers acts as a kind of compendium to some of the most fascinating figures in our history, from the beginnings of early civilization to the upheavals of the Second World War. The book's short entries are meant to be succinct and accessible, to provide a wide-ranging view of our past across the globe. They also represent just a toe's dip into the huge pool of numbers and history, a subject immeasurably vast and chasm-like. Our hope, nonetheless, is to package the past slightly differently, to provide a book that bears witness to man's many achievements and misdemeanours, all told through the powerful medium of numbers.

Emma Marriott

32 EDIBLE GRASSES

Some 10,000 years ago, most of the world's edible grasses (32 out of 56) – cereals like rice, wheat, barley and corn – grew wild in an area known as the Fertile Crescent. In the Americas and Africa, only four varieties grew, and in Western Europe just one (oats). Small wonder, then, that the world's first farming communities began to develop in this great arc of territory, located in and around the Euphrates and Tigris rivers, running through present-day western Syria, southern Turkey, Iraq, Kuwait, Lebanon and the western fringes of Iran.

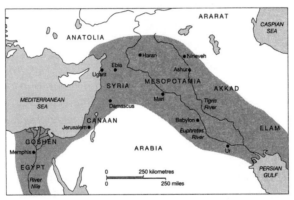

The Fertile Crescent, 10,000–4,500 BCE

The region's rich resources of edible plants, which included the wild strains of barley, wheat, lentils, onions and peas, were planted and cultivated by hunter-gatherers living on the plains and hills of the Fertile Crescent. Also plentiful were wild animals suited for domestication – goats, sheep, pigs and cattle (four of the five most important domesticated species; the fifth is the horse). This, combined with a climate that initially had sufficient rainfall to support farming without artificial irrigation, provided the vital prerequisites for crop

11

cultivation, the surplus of which eventually enabled people to settle in one place, develop technical skills, and evolve into the world's earliest civilizations.

700 Pictographic Symbols

The first known system of writing was developed in Sumer, the world's earliest civilization of southern Mesopotamia, situated in the Fertile Crescent. Early forms of farming had led to permanent settlement in Sumer somewhere between 5500 and 4000 BCE. These farming settlements had grown into small towns, and by 3000 BCE a number of city-states had developed, the largest Uruk, with a population of 40,000.

Each Sumerian city had its own temple precinct that was a place of worship as well as an administrative and governmental centre. These temples stored and distributed community food rations, organized labour for public works, and controlled the trade in raw materials like tin from Afghanistan and copper from Cyprus.

To manage and record this complex system, the Sumerians developed writing, the earliest examples found on clay tablets from Uruk dated 3300 BCE. This early form of writing is made up of pictographic symbols, over 700 of them, and was probably in use well before 3300 BCE, practised by a small circle of Sumerian bureaucrats, largely for purposes of book-keeping.

Eventually Sumerian writing spread to Babylonia, Assyria and Persia, Among other places, and it gradually evolved into a series of more abstract symbols represented by simplified wedge-shaped signs (the script's name, 'cuneiform', means 'wedge-shaped'). It remained in use for nearly 3,000 years, long after Uruk was sacked in 2000 BCE, after which Sumer came under Amorite rule.

60 Minutes and 60 Seconds

The demands of a complex administrative system in Sumer also led to developments in mathematics and time. Their counting system was based on the number sixty, which still rules the way we measure time. They divided their hours into sixty minutes and their minutes into sixty seconds. From this we also get the 360-degree circle. The Sumerians devised a seven-day week, naming five days after the five known planets – our Mercury, Venus, Mars, Jupiter and Saturn – and the other two after the Moon and Sun.

82 Bluestones at Stonehenge

Built between 3100 and 1500 BCE in Wiltshire, England, Stonehenge is a circular arrangement of massive upright stones surrounded by a large earthen embankment. Its double circle of bluestone pillars and sandstone blocks was aligned with the rays of the midsummer sunrise, suggesting that Stonehenge was built as a place of worship.

Its eighty-two bluestones, weighing 4 tons each, were transported 240 km (150 miles) from south-western Wales, and some time later its thirty sandstone blocks, weighing around 50 tons each, were transported from 32 km (20 miles) away. With little or no direct evidence on how Stonehenge was constructed, how these massive blocks of stones were transported remains subject to debate. Some have suggested the use of wheels (as these existed), although it's doubtful wooden axles could have withstood the weight of the pillars. It seems likely that the Welsh bluestones were transported on boats and then loaded on sledges drawn by oxen or teams of men. Whichever the method, Stonehenge shows that prehistoric peoples were able to conceive, design and construct features of impressive size and complexity.

2.5 MILLION STONE BLOCKS OF THE GREAT PYRAMID

Of the three pyramids built by the Ancient Egyptians at Giza, the Great Pyramid stands the tallest at 146 metres (479 feet) tall. It was built as a tomb for the pharaoh Khufu (2589–2566 BCE) to provide for his afterlife as he, like all rulers of Egypt, was believed to be the divine incarnation of the sun-god Ra. The steps of a pyramid were thought to provide a 'stairway to the gods' for the deceased pharaoh and its flared shape resembled the rays of the sun. Khufu's Great Pyramid was different in that it did not have stepped sides but was originally clad in smooth, polished limestone so that it reflected the sun's rays, making it visible for miles around – a fitting tribute to Khufu and Ra.

The workforce for this immense structure comprised about 20,000 labourers and 6,000 craftsmen. Taking around twenty years to build, the conundrum has always been how these immensely heavy stone blocks (2.5 million in the case of the Great Pyramid) were moved in a region where the wheel, crane and pulley were unknown. Some people believe the blocks were carried on rafts on the River Nile from quarries hundred of miles away, others that they came from nearby limestone quarries or that some of the blocks were formed like a kind of concrete in wooden moulds at the site, and then moved using only sleds and levers. Recent investigations of the Great Pyramid have revealed that the blocks may have been hauled up ramps that spiralled up inside the Pyramid, and then were blocked off once the Pyramid was completed.

30 Egyptian Dynasties

The Great Pyramid was constructed during an earlier period of Ancient Egypt's 3,000-year civilization, formed along the Nile valley in the north-east of Africa from around 3200 BCE. The pharaohs are grouped into thirty dynasties, and these in turn are grouped into three main periods known as the Old, Middle and New Kingdoms. These lasted from about 2575 to 30 BCE, when Egypt became part of the Roman Empire.

25th Dynasty

During the 25th Dynasty, Egypt was ruled by kings from the ancient African kingdom of Kush, situated in what is now the Republic of Sudan. In around 727 BCE, the Kushites had conquered all of Egypt and ruled as pharaohs for a century, until about 654 BCE.

70 Days of Mummification

The Egyptians practised the art of mummification, preserving people and sacred animals for the afterlife. The best technique took seventy days and involved removing the internal organs and pulling out the brain through the nose using an iron hook. The body was then dried using a mixture of salts called natron, its cavity packed with fragrant substances and resin-soaked linen and sawdust, and then wrapped in layers of linen bandages. Amulets were placed within the layers and the mummy placed in a human-shaped coffin.

20 TIMES THE SIZE OF ANCIENT EGYPT

Emerging in the fertile lower valley of the River Indus, in modern-day Pakistan and India, the Indus Valley civilization lasted from 2500 to around 1700 BCE. Evolving into a highly developed urban civilization, at its peak it had settlements spread across nearly 1.3 million square km (500,000 square miles). Compared with Ancient Egypt's 63,000 square km (24,000 square miles), the Indus Empire was by far the more extensive, twenty times the size of Egypt.

Yet before 1921, when archaeologists first unearthed remains in the Indus city of Harappa, nothing was known about this civilization. Even today, its script, which uses over 400 different signs, has only been partly deciphered, so many important questions about the Indus remain unanswered.

What is known is that Indus settlements comprised at least two large cities, Harappa and Mohenjo-daro (each with a population of 30,000–40,000), along with more than a hundred towns and villages. Cities and towns were built around a grid pattern of streets and were serviced by some of the most advanced plumbing and drainage systems in the world (in Mohenjo-daro, every domestic compound was provided with a brick culvert toilet, connected to brick-lined sewers running under the streets).

24 ANGULAS EQUALS A HASTA

The conformity of urban planning found in Indus cities was mirrored in its standardization of everything from pots and everyday tools to writing and weights. For a unit of measurement, the Indus used the 'hasta', which represented the length of a forearm measured out to the extended middle finger (about 45 cm/18 inches). A universal measurement of mankind, it equals 24 'angulas' and was akin to the cubit used in Sumeria.

282 LAWS

A name inseparably linked with the empire of Babylon is its sixth king Hammurabi (*c.* 1795–1750 BCE). Under his rule Babylon reached the peak of its influence, holding sway across the entire plain of Mesopotamia. Hammurabi is famed for instituting the world's first set of laws, known as the Hammurabi Code. This was a record of existing laws set up for the public to view. Partial copies exist on a large human-sized 'stele' (stone pillar) and various clay tablets. Its 282 articles of law deal comprehensively with a range of issues from wages and divorce to military service and laws about slavery (on which, like every other ancient civilization, Babylonian society relied). The best-known law is its 'eye for an eye' provision – 'If a man destroy the eye of another man, they shall destroy his eye' – although the punishment was reduced if it were a slave or a commoner who had been harmed.

THE 7 WONDERS OF THE ANCIENT WORLD

The pyramids built by the Ancient Egyptians at Giza were known as one of the Seven Wonders of the Ancient World. Observers living in Ancient Greece compiled various lists of the most spectacular man-made structures in the world, and the eventual list comprised:

1 Pyramids of Giza – built in around 2600 BCE, these are the only wonder that survive.

2 Hanging Gardens of Babylon – a towering stepped garden said to have been built by the Babylonian king Nebuchadnezzar II in modern-day Iraq in around 600 BCE. Many scholars believe that the gardens were a fictional creation.

3 Statue of Zeus at Olympia – this large statue graced the temple at Olympia for more than eight centuries from the mid-fifth century BCE.

4 Temple of Artemis at Ephesus – a Greek temple dedicated to the goddess Artemis, located in Ephesus, Turkey. It was rebuilt three times before its eventual destruction in 401.

5 Mausoleum of Halicarnassus – a tomb built in around 350 BCE at Halicarnassus in Turkey for Mausolus, a governor in the Persian Empire, and Artemisia II of Caria.

6 Colossus of Rhodes – a huge bronze statue built at Rhodes harbour. Completed in around 280 BCE, it was, at 30 metres (100 feet) high, the tallest statue in the ancient world.

7 Pharos of Alexandria – a lighthouse built for Ptolemy II of Egypt between 280 and 247 BCE on the island of Pharos, off Alexandria.

10,000 CLAY TABLETS

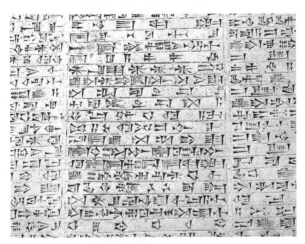

A Hittite cuneiform tablet

The Hittites were a powerful Bronze Age people who ruled regions now in Turkey and Syria for over a thousand years. Their empire, which reached its greatest extent between 1600 and 1200 BCE, easily rivalled the size and strength of the Babylonian and Egyptian empires. And yet before the twentieth century virtually nothing was known about the Hittites. It was only after the discovery in 1906 of some 10,000 clay tablets in the ruins of the ancient Hittite city of Khattushash (near Bogaz Koi) in Turkey that historians began to learn more about this warrior people.

As the tablets were in cuneiform writing, using Babylonian spelling but in the Hittite language, it took archaeologists nearly twenty years to translate them. Once deciphered, they revealed much about the social structure, politics, religion and economy of the Hittites. From these and just a few other documents, historians learned that the Hittites were wild tribesmen who not long after 3000 BCE swept into Anatolia (Asia Minor) from the north. A mainly agricultural society (bee-keeping was a major activity), the Hittites were also famous soldiers and one of the earliest people to fight and hunt on horseback. At its peak, their empire encompassed Syria almost to Canaan (modern-day Israel) and competition over Syria led to a famous battle between the Egyptian pharaoh Rameses II and the Hittite king Muwatallis at Qadesh, in around 1300 BCE.

1ST TO PRODUCE IRON

It is thought that the Hittites were the first civilization to produce iron on a large scale, using it for tools and weaponry. Producing iron from around 2500 BCE, the Hittites also in around 1400 BCE invented a smelting and cementation process to make iron stronger. Most other civilizations didn't use iron on this scale until several centuries later.

A MAZE OF 1,300 ROOMS

The Palace of Knossos

The Palace of Knossos, situated on Crete's northern coast, was the biggest of four magnificent palaces built by the Minoans. Established in around 1700 BCE, the palaces formed the centre of four small kingdoms in Crete. At five storeys high, Knossos contained a maze of around 1,300 rooms made up of living spaces, places of worship and entertainment, workshops and storerooms, all built around a central courtyard. Its complex layout may have given rise to the later Greek legend of the Labyrinth, where King Minos kept the Minotaur (a monster, half man and half bull) in an underground maze.

Knossos and the other Cretan palaces of Mallia, Phaistos and Kakros were built from the wealth generated by the Minoans' extensive trade in olive oil, wine and cloth throughout the Mediterranean. Emerging in around 3000 BCE, the Minoans were the first civilization to appear in Europe, leaving behind not only great palaces, but also fine pottery and metalwork.

The collapse of the Minoan civilization in around 1450 BCE enabled Mycenaeans from mainland Greece to occupy Crete and take over Minoan sea trade. They set up colonies in Rhodes, Cyprus and the south-west coast of Anatolia.

General turmoil in the Aegean then led to the sudden collapse of Mycenae in around 1120 BCE. By the time of the Ancient Greeks, the Minoan and Mycenaean civilizations were remembered as a lost and golden land, spawning myths and legends that include the Mycenaean sacking of Troy as depicted by the Greek poet Homer in his *Iliad*.

12,000 SHELLFISH

In the ancient era, the colour purple (also called Tyrian or imperial purple) was produced from the gland of various species of marine molluscs, notably the murex. It took around 12,000 of these molluscs to yield just 1.5 grams of purple dye, a process so laborious that purple textiles sold for extremely high prices. Purple was thus a prized luxury item associated with royalty and power, as favoured by later eminent Romans and the priesthood.

The Phoenicians, a great commercial and colonial power of the eastern Mediterranean, were famed for their purple textiles (indeed the name Phoenicia is derived from the Greek word for 'purple'). Ancient authors even wrote about the hideous stench that emanated from large vats of molluscs left to decompose in the Phoenician city of Tyre.

Trade, particularly in luxury items like purple textiles, glassware and gold and silver ornaments, formed the cornerstone of Phoenician prosperity, which reached its peak in around 1000 BCE. A maritime power, Phoenicia also established colonies in Cyprus and all along the African coast, notably Carthage in 814 BCE. By 322 BCE, Tyre had been sacked and Phoenicia was incorporated into the Greek world of Alexander the Great (see pages 35–36).

100,000 Oracle Bones

Much of what we know about China's first known dynasty, the Shang, comes from its sophisticated pictographic writing system, developed in around 1500 BCE. Made up of over 2,000 symbols, it was inscribed on more than 100,000 oracle bones (mostly turtle shells or shoulder blades of oxen) found in the Shang capital of Anyang, southwest of what is now Beijing.

Shang kings tried to predict the future by inscribing questions into a bone, then striking it with a red-hot bronze poker so as to create a pattern of cracks. These cracks would be interpreted by diviners and the answers recorded on the bone. Most questions concerned the weather, crops, hunting or war, but there are also questions of a more domestic nature, such as advice on how to cure a king's toothache.

In the absence of written records, little is known about life in China before 1766 BCE, when tradition dates the birth of the Shang. Some 13,000 years ago it is thought that people living near the Yangtze River in China were gathering and eating rice, and there is evidence of farming in northern China above the floodplains of the Yellow River from about 5000 BCE. The discovery of stone tools and bronze smelters has suggested to some historians that an earlier civilization, the Xia dynasty, emerged in the Yellow River valley in around 2100 BCE, but others consider this a legend.

12 Signs of the Zodiac

Babylonians scanned the stars in a bid to understand their destinies, and this drove developments in science and astronomy. By 1000 BCE, the prediction of lunar eclipses was possible, and the path of certain planets was plotted with surprising accuracy. At some point in the first millennium BCE, Babylonian astronomers divided the plane of the Earth's orbit and the apparent annual path of the Sun across the celestial sphere into twelve equal zones (each of 30 degrees, to make a complete circle of 360 degrees). This concept was taken into Egyptian, Hindu and Greek thought and beyond, and the relevant symbols of the zodiac are strikingly similar to those of the Mesopotamians – Gu Anna (Bull of Heaven) is Taurus, Mastabba Bagal (Great Twins) is Gemini, Girtab (Scorpion) is Scorpio, and so on.

THE 10 LOST TRIBES OF ISRAEL

In around 722 BCE, ten of the twelve Israelite tribes were forced out of the ancient northern kingdom of Israel by the Assyrians. These tribes were gradually assimilated by other people and thus lost to history (hence the 'Ten Lost Tribes of Israel'). Some religious groups have Messianic hopes for the future restoration of the long-lost tribes, others today claim descent from the tribes, whilst many maintain the story is purely mythical.

The legend is based on the conquest of the Assyrian king Sargon II (722–705 BCE), who had made Israel an Assyrian province, exiling 30,000 Israelites in the process. The Assyrians, who had broken away from Babylonian rule in the fourteenth century BCE, were fierce warriors and innovative weapon makers. By the seventh century BCE they had built from their northern Mesopotamian origin a huge empire that stretched from the Persian Gulf up to and including Egypt. One of their last great kings, Ashurbanipal (668–627 BCE), constructed in its capital Nineveh the Middle East's first organized library, containing thousands of clay tablets. Some 20,720 of these cuneiform tablets are stored in the British Museum in London.

Land of the 7 Rivers

The most ancient of the Hindu scriptures, the *Rigveda*, refers to a geographical region of India, in the upper Indus valley, which it calls 'the Land of the Seven Rivers'. Composed at some point between 1400 and 1000 BCE, the *Rigveda* forms the first part of a collection of Hindu hymns and sacred writings, called the 'Veda', meaning 'knowledge'. They are written in Sanskrit, which evolved into several modern spoken languages, including Hindi.

Vedic forms of belief are seen as the precursor to Hinduism. The poems and hymns of the Vedas praise a wide range of gods such as Agni (personifying fire) and Indra (rain), as well as Mitra (friendship) and Vach (speech). Central to Vedic worship would be the performance of sacrifices, and use of the hallucinogenic juice of the soma plant (as yet unidentified). In modern Hinduism the Vedas are less influential than other texts, although certain Vedic hymns are always recited as temple rituals, ceremonies for the dead or traditional weddings.

1.8 Million Words

The Sanskrit epic poem known as the *Mahabharata* is the longest work of literature in the world. Dating back to the first millennium BCE, the text reached its final form in around 400 CE. It consists of a mass of mythological and moralistic stories, arranged around a central narrative about a feud between two royal cousins. Divided into eighteen parvans, or sections, it is made up of almost 100,000 couplets (around 1.8 million words in total) and is about eight times the combined length of Homer's *Iliad* and *Odyssey*. It is regarded as a major source of information on the development of Hinduism and is regarded by Hindus as a text about dharma (Hindu moral law).

40-TON COLOSSAL HEADS

The Olmecs, the first recognized civilization to emerge in the Americas, were exceptional artists whose enduring legacy are the enormous sculpted heads they created – seventeen are known in locations along Mexico's Gulf Coast. Each head, topped with a helmet or headdress, has a distinctive look and personality, and they are thus thought to be representations of individual rulers. The largest, standing at 3 metres (10 feet), was discovered at La Cobata.

Like other ancient monuments of this stature, the transportation and creation of these huge structures is a remarkable feat. The basalt boulders used for the heads were transported from as far away as 80 km (50 miles) by rafts on rivers, sledges, and using levers. Their carvers used simple stone hammers, as metal tools were unknown.

The heads formed part of large ceremonial sites, often alongside large earth pyramids. Emerging in around 1500 BCE, the Olmecs were to influence the art of later central American cultures, including the Maya (see pages 57–58), who succeeded them in around 400 BCE.

THE 7 HILLS OF ROME

The ancient city of Rome is said to have been built on a group of seven hills: the Palatine (the central hill), Aventine, Capitoline, Quirinal, Viminal, Esquiline and Caelian (although the last four hills are really promontories of an ancient volcanic ridge). These hills and the land around them were first settled by the Latins, Etruscans and Sabines. (The Etruscan civilization dominated central Italy in around the seventh and sixth centuries BCE; their art and architecture would leave their mark on Rome.)

Founded, according to Roman tradition, in 753 BCE, the city's first king and founding father was Romulus. In the myths of Rome's foundation, his quarrel with his twin brother Remus over the siting of the new city led to the death of Remus. Romulus was followed by another six kings of both Latin and Etruscan origin. Legend has it that the tyrannical rule of Lucius Tarquinius Superbus was overthrown in 509 BCE by a group of noblemen, after which Rome was set up as a republic.

The power and fame of Rome have led cities around the world to emulate the origins of 'the eternal city': Jerusalem, Lisbon, Barcelona, Istanbul and Moscow are among others that claim to stand on seven hills.

⅕ OF THE WORLD'S POPULATION

The Persian Empire extended 2,500 miles (4,000 km), from northern India in the east to Turkey in the west, one of the largest, richest and most powerful empires the world had seen. Much of this vast realm, also called the Achaemenian Empire after its founder king Achaemenes, was created in little more than a decade by Cyrus II. After coming to power in 559 BCE, Cyrus conquered the Medes (Indo-Europeans living in northern Iraq), acquiring Assyria in the process. His armies seized the Ionian Greek cities, captured Babylon, then expanded the empire to the borders of India in 529 BCE, by which time his empire ruled over a fifth of the world's population.

2,400-KM ROYAL ROAD

By the time of Darius I, 'the Great' (522–486 BCE), the Persian Empire also took in Egypt. To control this huge domain, Darius introduced an effective system of administration and taxes, an imperial postal network, and in 500 BCE built a road spanning 2,400 km (1,500 miles), from Susa in modern Iran to Ephesus in Turkey. It's 100-plus relay stations provided lodgings for travellers; the journey usually took ninety days, but the fastest couriers covered it in a week. Indeed the Greek historian Herodotus remarked: 'Neither snow nor rain nor heat nor gloom of night stays these couriers from the swift completion of their appointed rounds' – a quote associated today with the United States Postal Service.

3 LANGUAGES

The life story of Darius I is carved into a rock at Behistun, in modern Iran. Inscribed in three languages, Old Persian, Elamite and Babylonian, the stone was rediscovered in the nineteenth century and enabled scholars to unlock the other two languages (as Old Persian was decipherable from modern Persian). They could thus translate the cuneiforms of ancient Mesopotamia.

1 GOD

By the time the Jews had returned to Jerusalem during the Persian conquests of Babylon and Canaan, they had come to see themselves as the chosen people of a single, all-powerful God, the 'one true God' who, according to scriptures, had appeared to the herdsman Abraham in the early half of the second millennium BCE.

This worship of one god, known as monotheism, contrasted with the worship and belief in multiple deities, typical during the Bronze and Iron Ages, and with the pantheon of Ancient Greek and Roman gods. Belief in a single, universal God who has a personal relationship with everyone who believes in Him would influence the religions of Christianity and Islam – in Muslim tradition, Abraham (Ibrahim) was the 'Father of the Prophets', and in the Bible, Jesus is descended from Abraham.

Women Own 40 Per Cent of the Land

Women in Sparta, a dominant city-state of ancient Greece, enjoyed a power and status unrecognized in the rest of the ancient world. The Greek philosopher Aristotle tells us that women owned 40 per cent of the land in Sparta, referring most probably to a later period of Spartan history when the male population was in decline. Nonetheless, it is a remarkable figure, particularly when global estimates today show that less than 10 per cent of women around the world own land.

Situated in Laconia in the southern Peloponnese, Sparta had by around 700 BCE become the leading military power in ancient Greece. Its population comprised a large slave class known as helots, freemen and Spartan citizens, whose men from the age of seven were required to undergo rigorous military training and education designed to encourage discipline and physical toughness. This elite military force enabled the city-state to lead the successful Greek resistance against the Persians in the Greco-Persian wars, entering into a protracted conflict with Athens and emerging dominant in Greece and the Aegean in 404 BCE.

Within the unique social system of Sparta, geared largely

towards military training and excellence and underpinned by its large slave force, Spartan women enjoyed a freedom remarkable in the Greek world. They could inherit property and expect to receive half the share of what a son would receive. While part if not all the shares came in the form of a dowry when they married, it still let Spartan women gain significantly more wealth than Athenian women.

Unlike women in Athens, who were largely confined to the homes of their fathers or husbands, Spartan women could walk freely about the city and drive chariots, they could run businesses, take an informal role in politics, and even exercise like their male counterparts by performing gymnastics in the nude (deeply shocking other Greeks).

Spartan law even forbade marriage until a girl had reached her late teens or twenties. This was done to ensure she gave birth to healthy children (her primary role in Spartan society), but in effect it ensured she avoided the hazards of early pregnancy and had a greater chance of living longer (unlike women in other Greek cities whose average life span was 34.6, some ten years fewer than that of men).

4 PERIODS OF ANCIENT GREECE

The history of ancient Greece is often divided into four periods, starting with the Archaic (*c.* 750–480 BCE), when the city-states grew in power, the Olympic Games were held and the Greeks established colonies in Italy, Gaul, Spain, Libya and around the Black Sea. Classical Greece (*c.* 480–336 BCE) is known as the greatest age of ancient Greece. A united Greece defeated the Persians (see page 31), the Parthenon was built in celebration and democracy was established. The Hellenistic Period (*c.* 336–146 BCE) marks the conquest of Greece by Philip II of Macedonia and the subsequent rule of Alexander the Great. During this period, Aristotle composed many of his great works, and Greek culture and language was exported to Hellenistic kingdoms like Egypt and Syria. The Roman Period (from 146 BCE) saw Greece incorporated into the Roman Empire.

Olympic Games Every 4 Years

From around 730 BCE, towns in Greece had grown in power and prosperity, with the city-states of Athens, Sparta, Corinth and Thebes emerging as dominant by the time of Greece's Archaic Period (750–480 BCE). Often at war, these city-states met every four years at Greece's most prestigious sporting event, the Olympic Games.

First recorded in 776 BCE, the earliest games consisted of a 180-metre (200-yard) running race, although by 632 BCE they included wrestling, boxing, pentathlon, chariot and horse racing. The games lasted for five days and attracted thousands of spectators from all over Greece (although this was strictly a men-only affair: women were not allowed to watch). As a festival of religious importance, the games closed with feasting and the sacrifice of one hundred oxen to the god Zeus.

The four-year period from the start of one Olympic Games to the start of the next was known as the Olympiad, and formed the basis of the ancient Greek calendar. The first Olympiad would have lasted from 776 to 772 BCE. As each city-state had a different calendar, this became a crucial means to measure dates and time spans.

ATHENIAN ARMY, 9,000–10,000; PERSIAN ARMY, 20,000–100,000

Despite being seriously outnumbered by the Persians, the Athenian army gained a remarkable victory at the Battle of Marathon, a watershed in the Greco-Persian Wars. Previously the armies of the Persian ruler, Darius I (see page 30), had been successful in their campaign to capture Ionian Greek settlements, after they had revolted against Persian rule in 499 BCE.

Persian fortunes would switch, however, when in 490 BCE they met the Athenian army at Marathon, some 40 km (24 miles) from Athens. Sources suggest there were 9,000 to 10,000 Athenian soldiers, while estimates for the Persian army range from 20,000 to 100,000 infantrymen, with possibly 1,000 cavalry. In battle, the soldiers of the Athenian army, with a deliberately weak centre and reinforced flanks, charged the Persian army, luring the best Persian fighters to the centre. The Persians were subsequently enveloped by the Athenian army and slaughtered in great numbers.

Ten years later, Darius's son Xerxes mounted a much larger invasion of Greece (the Greek historian Herodotus claimed he mustered 5.2 million men, an exaggerated figure, but his army was huge nonetheless). The Persians succeeded in invading and burning Athens in 480 BCE, but were ultimately defeated by allied Athenian and Spartan forces in the same year and 479 BCE, decisively ending the Persian threat to Greece.

MALE CITIZENS OVER THE AGE OF 20

In the fifth century of Classical Greece, Athens successfully repulsed a Spartan invasion. Then in a bid to avoid tyrannical rule by local rich landowners, the people of Athens established the world's first democracy (the Greek *demokratia* means 'rule of the people').

The principal organ of democracy was the popular assembly, open to all male citizens over twenty. This amounted to around 30,000 out of Athens's total population of 120,000–180,000. Men born outside of Athens, women and slaves (and there were probably two slaves for every Athenian free male) were excluded. The popular assembly elected a council of 500 who ruled Athens day-to-day, although the full assembly would also meet, with around 6,000 Athenian men attending most weeks. This, the world's first democracy based on direct citizen rule, survived in Athens for nearly 200 years.

500,000–700,000 PAPYRUS ROLLS

Alexander the Great, son of Philip II of Macedonia, conquered Greece in 339 BCE. A student of the great Macedonian philosopher Aristotle, Alexander's fine armies invaded Persia, defeated King Darius at the Battle of Issus in 333 BCE, swept through Syria and went on to create the largest empire the world had ever seen, with conquered territories ranging from Egypt to north-west India.

While in Egypt, Alexander founded the city of Alexandria in 332 BCE, which, under the patronage of the Ptolemaic dynasty, became a major centre for Hellenistic culture. The city boasted the 91-metre (300-foot) Pharos lighthouse at its port, grand buildings in the Greek style, and a museum and library, perhaps the largest in the ancient world, and said to contain copies of every book printed in Greek, in the form of between 500,000 and 700,000 papyrus rolls.

The library formed part of the Museum of Alexandria, a research institute where many of the most famous thinkers of the ancient world studied. These included Euclid, who invented modern geometry and wrote works on prime numbers, perspective and conic sections. The mathematician and engineer Archimedes is thought to have been his pupil. Another Alexandrian, Eratosthenes, was the first man to measure the circumference of the Earth, while another, Hero, is said to have made a model steam engine. The library was eventually destroyed through several acts of fire and siege, continuing to some degree until 275 CE. Alexander the Great died, aged only thirty-three, in 323 BCE, with much of his empire carved up and ruled by Macedonian generals, including the Ptolemaic dynasty, which lasted in Egypt for another 300 years until it was annexed by Rome in 30 BCE.

3 Orders of Greek Architecture

Three orders of ancient Greek architecture: Doric, Ionic, and Corinthian

Greek art, particularly sculpture and architecture, dominated the art of the Western world right up to the nineteenth century. Stylistically, ancient Greek architecture is divided into three 'orders' (whose names reflect their origin): the Doric order, with sturdy columns and undecorated capitals; the Ionic order, with taller, slender columns and carved 'volutes' (spirals) decorating its capitals; and the Corinthian order with a deeper capital shaped like a *krater*, a mixing bowl, decorated with acanthus leaves and splayed tendrils.

The Age of 80 (or Thereabouts)

Dates for the birth and death of Siddhartha Gautama, the sage who became known as Buddha ('the enlightened one'), are hard to pin down. As there are no written records from his lifetime or even four or five centuries later, the best that historians can say is that he lived at some point between

563 and 483 BCE. According to one source, the Buddha announced at the age of eighty that he would soon abandon his earthly body.

Born in northern India, Gautama came from a wealthy background, but at the age of twenty-nine he decided to give up his riches to search for the meaning of life. Sitting beneath a bodhi tree, he found enlightenment and thereafter dedicated the rest of his life to teaching others what he had learned. The central theme of Buddhism and its teachings (the Dharma) is that all phenomena are linked by a central chain of dependency, the world's suffering is caused by selfish desire, and the goal of life is to reach a state of 'nirvana', literally the 'blowing out of desire'. Buddhism would eventually spread after his death to parts of Asia that included present-day Sri Lanka, Thailand, Burma and Tibet. From the third century CE it travelled to China, and then to Korea and Japan.

Though the date of the Buddha's death is uncertain, we know that his body was cremated and his ashes placed in eight urns buried in earth mounds. Two centuries later the Maurya Emperor of India, Ashoka (see page 48), would excavate these urns and subdivide them to create 84,000 memorial shrines to Buddha.

THE 5 CONFUCIAN CLASSICS

The basic texts of the Chinese philosophy Confucianism are the Five Confucian Classics. Including the *Book of Changes*, or *I Ching* (which sees the cosmos as the interaction between two energies, yin and yang), the Confucian classics illustrate the core value and belief systems of Confucianism. They are believed to have been written or edited by the most celebrated

Chinese philosopher Confucius (c. 551–479 BCE) during the Zhou dynasty (which ruled China from the eleventh century BCE until 256 BCE).

Confucianism was to become the official state ideology of the Han in China (see page 43), it saw a revival during the Tang Dynasty (see pages 59–60), and there are currently upwards of six million followers in the world, mostly in China, Korea, Japan and Vietnam. Its basic concepts are ethical ones: filial piety, decorum, love for one's fellows, virtue and the ideal of the superior man.

8,000 Life-Size Terracotta Figures

Emperor Qin Shi Huang's Terracotta Army

In 1974, farmers were digging a well in Xi'an, China, when they broke into a pit containing 6,000 life-size terracotta figures. Further excavation in 1976 revealed two further pits and to date nearly 8,000 terracotta figures have been found (although many remain buried).

The figures, known as the Terracotta Army, were buried with the first Emperor of China, Qin Shi Huang, in around 210 BCE, their purpose to protect him in his afterlife. They include warriors, chariots and horses, and are modelled in extraordinary detail, with even the soles of their shoes given fine tread patterns. They vary in height, uniform and hairstyle, according to their rank.

Qin Shi Huang was the first emperor of the Qin dynasty (Chinese rulers would bear the title emperor for the next 2,000 years). This dynasty, China's first united empire, was formed in 221 BCE and ended in 206 BCE (the name 'China' is derived from Qin). The Qin instituted a rigid form of government, establishing a unified system of writing, weights and measures. As a shield against wandering tribes to the north, they also created the Great Wall of China (linking earlier defensive walls), whose building claimed the lives of hundreds of thousands of its workers. A total of 300,000 soldiers and 500,000 civilians were involved in the construction of the original Great Wall.

HANNIBAL'S 37 ELEPHANTS

The Carthaginian general Hannibal emerged during the Punic Wars during a series of clashes fought between the Roman Republic and Carthage beginning in 264 BCE. Carthage, situated on the coast of modern Tunisia, had established itself as a major trading centre and its founding of colonies in North Africa, Spain and Sicily had brought it into conflict first with Greece, then with Rome.

To launch the second Punic War (218–201 BCE), Hannibal, the commander of Spain, took an army of about 30,000 men and thirty-seven elephants across the Pyrenees and Alps into northern Italy. (Carthage had deployed war elephants to great effect during the first Punic War.) The march was perilous, and only one of the elephants survived, apparently named Surus ('the Syrian'), an elephant that Hannibal himself often rode.

In Italy, Hannibal inflicted a series of defeats on the Romans, including the Battle of Cannae in 216 BCE in which some 50,000–70,000 Romans fell (one of Rome's most significant defeats). But he could not deal the final blow, and at last Carthage fell to the Romans in 146 BCE, when they massacred 200,000 and sold the remaining 50,000 as slaves.

Thereafter, the Roman Republic grew in strength, through the capture of Carthaginian colonies and, through four Macedonian wars, the extension of its rule into Macedonia, Greece and part of Gaul. Roman ambitions in the east however, were effectively finished off at the Battle of Carrhae in 53 BCE after the Roman army fell to the mounted bowmen of the Parthians (who from their base in north-east Persia had built an empire stretching from what is now south-eastern Turkey to eastern Iran). Some 44,000 Roman soldiers were routed; only 10,000 escaped alive.

1 IN 3 GAULS SLAIN

Between 58 and 51 BCE, the Roman general Julius Caesar waged a series of campaigns against several Gallic tribes that extended Roman rule over the whole of Gaul (present-day France and Belgium). Ruthlessly fought, the wars killed around 1.2 million on the battlefield, and enslaved or starved

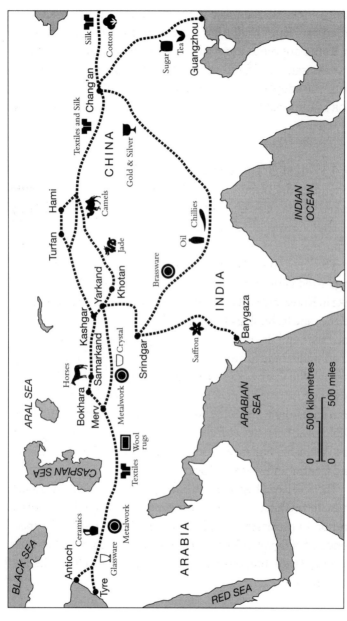

The Silk Road and the goods that were traded between the East and the West

to death a similar number – one in three people in Gaul were killed or disappeared. After a period of civil war, Julius Caesar in Rome appointed himself dictator for life, after which he was assassinated, famously on the Ides (15th) of March 44 BCE. His adopted son Octavian subsequently ruled from 27 BCE as Imperial Rome's first emperor, renamed as Augustus.

6,437-KM SILK ROAD

Extending 6,437 km (4,000 miles), this ancient caravan route linked China with the West. It took its name from the trade by which Chinese merchants carried silks to the Western world from around 100 BCE.

The Han dynasty of China (206 BCE–220 CE), with its organized central government, extended China's borders to take in Korea and parts of Vietnam. It made huge advances in art, science and technology (including the invention of paper and the compass), and also expanded the central Asian sections of the Silk Road trade route in around 114 BCE. This was achieved largely through the work of the imperial envoy Zhang Qian (220–114 BCE), whose reports of his travels to central Asia revealed to the Han emperors a part of the world previously unknown to them. Diplomatic relations with countries in central Asia (among them the Parthians) enhanced commercial relations between China and Central and Western Asia.

The Silk Road began in the old capital Chang'an (now Xi'an) in eastern China, crossing through north-west China, Persia and on to the eastern Mediterranean. Soon after the Roman conquest of Egypt in 30 BCE, trade and communication between Europe, Africa, the Middle East, India and China flourished as never before.

1,000 Paces

Some 400,00 km (250,000 miles) of road were built by the Romans to carry their troops, supplies and goods across their ever-expanding empire. The Romans developed a form of concrete to produce a waterproof surface, and many of their typically straight routes form the basis of the roads in use today. Milestones marked out many Roman roads, the modern 'mile' deriving from the Latin *mille passuum* (one thousand paces).

The 4 Gospels

Within the New Testament of the Christian Bible, there are four gospels (originally 'godspell' in Anglo-Saxon, a translation of *evangelium*, 'good news') – Matthew, Mark, Luke and John – apparently written by four of the twelve apostles. They contain information about the life of Jesus, along with an interpretation of his teachings.

According to the gospels, Jesus was born in Bethlehem, in Galilee, to Mary in the reign of the Roman emperor Augustus Caesar (27 BCE to 14 CE). In around 27 CE, Jesus began preaching to fellow Jews, speaking of a compassionate and merciful God and the fundamental principles of charity, sincerity and humility. His preaching antagonized the Jewish authorities, who brought him before the Roman governor, Pontius Pilate, who ordered his death by crucifixion. Three days after his crucifixion, the gospels claim he rose from the dead, proving to his followers that he was the Messiah or Christ.

Over the next two centuries, the beliefs of Jesus, as enshrined in the four gospels, spread around the Roman world. Mark was the first and shortest Gospel written (composed probably in the decade preceding 70 CE), and it's thought that Matthew and Luke used Mark as a source to write their gospels, as they are similar in form and content. The spread of Jesus's teachings was also aided in part by the letters of St Paul, a former tent maker from Asia Minor, who wrote thirteen of the twenty-seven books in the New Testament. His letters to Christian communities date from no more than twenty years after the death of Jesus and are the earliest Christian writings to survive.

Despite widespread persecution by Roman authorities of followers of the dangerous cult of Christianity (most intensely under Decius in 250 CE and Diocletian in 303–311 CE), by 381 CE Christianity had become the official religion of the Roman Empire, thereafter spreading throughout Europe and beyond.

A CENTURY EQUALS 100 MEN?

The Romans possessed a powerful army, the bedrock of their empire. Its smallest unit was a century, which was made up, not of one hundred men as you would expect, but eighty men. Six centuries would make up a cohort and nine cohorts a legion (along with cavalry, engineers and officers). At the time of Emperor Hadrian (117–138 CE) the Roman army fielded twenty-eight legions.

Military garrisons were positioned throughout the Empire, and this led to a process of cultural exchange and assimilation between the Roman military and local populations. Indeed, the Roman army absorbed many of its fighting men from its occupied lands: out of the 380,000 men that made up Emperor Hadrian's army, 154,000 troops were supported by 215,000 auxiliaries (infantry and cavalry), who came mostly from Rome's conquered lands.

⅛ of the Roman Army

The Roman occupation of Britain, following the invasion of Emperor Claudius in 43 CE, spurred fierce opposition from Celtic tribes. For this reason, an eighth of the entire Roman army was needed to garrison Britain. In the first century CE, tribal revolts included the Iceni revolt in 60 CE, which under the leadership of Queen Boudicca destroyed the towns of Camulodunum (Colchester), London and Verulamium (St Albans), and almost ended Roman rule in Britain. Ultimately, the Romans failed to conquer the northern parts of Britain (they never even tried invading Ireland) and in 122 CE they built the defensive Hadrian's Wall to protect Roman Britain against Scotland's warlike Picts.

Collapse of Rome in Just 6 Decades

The Roman Empire, with territories in Europe, North Africa and the Middle East, reached its largest extent under Emperor Trajan (98–117 CE). It covered an area of 5 million square km (3.1 million square miles), accounting for between one-sixth and one-quarter of the world population.

In the end, the sheer size of the empire led to its downfall as its troops faced successive opposition from European and Asian enemies, notably in 260 CE when Emperor Valerian was defeated and imprisoned by the Persian Sassanid Empire. In 396 CE, the empire was again divided into east and west: the Eastern Roman Empire, from its renamed capital of Constantinople, thrived, whereas the Western Roman Empire was increasingly weakened by battles with migrating settlers from central Europe.

The end came remarkably fast. Beginning in 406, when Germanic tribes poured across the Rhine into Italy and Gaul, the Western Roman Empire was to collapse in just six decades. By 439, Carthage was lost to the Vandals, and by 452 the Roman Empire had lost a vast tract of its empire (including all of Britain and most of Spain). At the same time, Rome saw its population plummet by three-quarters and was itself sacked by Germanic tribes in 455 CE. By 476 CE, as the last Roman emperor, Romulus Augustus, abdicated, the Western Roman Empire had dissolved.

300,000 DEAD

In 451 CE, a decisive battle took place in the Champagne region of eastern France when a combined army of Roman and Visigoth forces confronted the Huns and their allies. The battle, one of the last military operations of the western Roman Empire, resulted in defeat for the Huns and their fearsome leader, Attila.

How many took part in the battle, and how many died, is unknown. Hydatius, a chronicler at the time, reported that 300,000 lay dead, but neither side could have fielded so many at the time. (In 450 CE, the Roman army in the west was roughly half its size of fifty years before.) Recent estimates suggest that the number of combatants could have been 100,000 in total, with Roman–Gothic forces approximately the same size as the Hunnic forces. The number killed can only be a guess, although sources say the battlefields were 'piled high with corpses'.

The defeat marked the end of the Hun advance into Gaul and heralded the expulsion of Attila's forces in Italy the following year. The Huns, a formidable nomadic race from central Asia, had swept into Europe at the end of the fourth century, displacing other Germanic tribes and pushing them further west into Europe. Their leader Attila, whom contemporary Christian writers dubbed 'the scourge of God', died in 453, and after the collapse of the Hunnic Empire the Slavs of eastern Europe (known by the Romans as the Scythians and Sarmatians) migrated westwards into the void the Huns left behind.

THE CONCEPT OF 0

The Gupta dynasty in India, which followed the Maurya Empire (321–185 BCE), is often called 'the Golden Age of India', as art, architecture and literature flourished during its long periods of peace and prosperity. The dynasty also produced great scholars, among them the mathematician–astronomer Aryabhata (476–550 CE). He is believed to have devised the invaluable concept of zero, using the word 'kha' ('emptiness') to mark 'zero' in tabular arrangements of digits. (The Western world did not stumble across the concept until several centuries later.)

In addition – and often wrongly attributed to the Arabs, who simply passed it on to the Europeans – the Guptas invented the 'Hindu–Arabic' method of writing numbers (which in the West evolved into the numbers 0, 1, 2, 3, 4, 5, 6, 7, 8, 9).

Constantinople's 2 Barrier Walls

The huge walls and fortifications that surrounded Constantinople (formerly the Greek city of Byzantium and now Istanbul) were pivotal features in late antiquity. They allowed the city and the Byzantine Empire to survive and prosper for over a thousand years, despite repeated attacks from all sides.

As Germanic invaders ravaged the Western Roman Empire, the city of Constantinople, capital of the Eastern Roman Empire (later to be known as the Byzantine Empire), continued to thrive. An inner early wall was built by the empire's first emperor Constantine (324–337 CE), and a double reinforcement added by Emperor Theodosius II (408–450 CE). Stretching for 22 km (14 miles), his inner walls were 4.5–6 metres thick and 12 metres high, the outer wall 2 metres thick and 8.5–9 metres tall.

These twin stone shields, along with the city's location on seven hills, set between the Golden Horn and Sea of Marmara, were deemed impregnable for any attacker, and the city withstood repeated attacks from Goths, Persians and Arabs right up to 1453, when it fell at last to the Ottoman Turks.

Over its thousand-year dominance, Constantinople, straddling Europe and Asia, flourished through commerce, its opulent art and architecture admired by all who visited. With Christianity its official religion, by 565 CE the Byzantine Empire stretched from Spain to North Africa and on to Persia. At the same time, the urban population had grown to half a million inhabitants, the largest, richest city in the Western world.

6 MILLION EUROS

In April 2005, an Antonov airplane landed in Ethiopia carrying the middle part of a 24-metre (78-ft), 160-ton obelisk. The top and bottom parts of the huge structure were later flown from Rome to Ethiopia. The whole operation cost the Italian government an estimated €6 million ($7.7 million).

Believed to be the largest and heaviest object ever transported by air, the obelisk was originally looted by Italian troops in 1937 and taken to Rome to commemorate the Italian conquest of Ethiopia. Despite a UN agreement in 1947 to return the obelisk to Ethiopia, it remained in Rome, standing for years outside the United Nations Food and Agriculture Organisation headquarters.

The ornately decorated obelisk is regarded as a fine example of architecture from the great trading empire of Aksum in the north-east of Africa (now a city of modern-day Ethiopia). Having overthrown the kingdom of Kush in 300 CE, the Aksum Empire remained a thriving commercial centre until the late 600s. With an empire that housed several wealthy cities, Aksum is famed for its huge granite obelisks (the tallest stands at 34 metres), which served a religious purpose prior to Aksum's conversion to Christianity in the fourth century CE.

AD 0

This book uses the culturally neutral dating BCE and CE ('before common era' / 'common era'). It succeeds the original Western dating system, AD or Anno Domini (in the year of the Lord) and BC or Before Christ, devised in 525 CE by a Scythian monk, Dionysius Exiguus. The AD years are counted from the year of Jesus Christ's birth, and as zero was then unknown to the West, Dionysius began his new Christian era as AD 1, not AD 0.

Working for Pope John I in Rome, Dionysius was attempting to calculate the Easter tables (Easter is a moveable feast in the Christian calendar) when he saw the opportunity to discard the old numbering system, Anno Diocletiani, in which years were counted from the beginning of the reign of Roman Emperor Diocletian, who ruled from 245 to 305 CE. (Diocletian had overseen the Empire's largest and bloodiest persecution of Christians, so it seemed inappropriate to commemorate him.)

While the consensus now agrees that Jesus was probably born between 7 and 3 BCE, Dionysius's new calendar is now the most widely used in the world. It didn't take off immediately, and became widespread only after the Anglo-Saxon monk Bede popularized the new dating system in his *Ecclesiastical History of the English People*, in 731. The Frankish king Charlemagne (see page 56) and his successors also helped to spread its use in Europe when it was adopted for dating acts of government throughout the Carolingian Empire.

In contrast, Muslims begin their calendar with the flight of Muhammad, the year of the Hijra (622 CE). The Jewish calendar is thought to have been influenced by the Babylonian calendar, and according to Jewish scriptures, dates back to 3761 BCE, when God created the world.

5 Pillars of Islam

The five pillars of Islam are the essential principles and prescribed acts of worship for the follower of Islam (Islam means 'surrender', as believers surrender to the will of their one God, Allah). The five pillars are: profession of the faith in a prescribed form; observance of ritual prayer (five obligatory prayer sequences each day, alongside non-obligatory prayers); giving charity to the poor; fasting for thirty days during the month of Ramadan; and the haj, the pilgrimage to Mecca.

These ritual observances and a code governing social behaviour were given to the prophet Muhammad, an Arab merchant living in Mecca, as a series of revelations, the first of which he received in 610 CE, in which he was told to proclaim the greatness of One Almighty God, Allah. These revelations were eventually collected in a book known as the Qur'an.

Muhammad began to preach these revelations, at first attracting few followers and meeting with hostility from some Meccan tribes, which led him to migrate to Medina in 622 CE (an event known as the Hijra, which marks the beginning of the Islamic calendar). Eventually his message of Islam gained a large number of supporters, and Muhammad returned to Mecca with some 10,000 followers.

By the time of his death in 632 CE, most of the Arab peninsula was under Islamic rule. Thereafter the new faith of Islam spread into Palestine, Sassanid Persia and Egypt. Arab armies under the Omayyad dynasty took control of the whole of North Africa and large parts of Asia, and repeatedly, but without success, tried to conquer Constantinople. Spain, previously under the Visigoths, fell to Islamic rule, although Arab armies failed to reach any further than Poitiers in France, where they were defeated by the Franks in 732 (see page 56).

Maintaining its emphasis on essential religious practices

and uncompromising monotheism, the religion that was initially taught by Muhammad to a small group of followers is now practised by more than 1.5 billion Muslims worldwide, from the Middle East, Africa and Europe to the Indian subcontinent, the Malay Peninsula and China.

X + Y = ?

During the Islamic conquests, new Islamic dynasties were set up to include, in around 750 CE, the Abbasid caliphate ('caliph' from the Arabic *kalifa*, 'successor'). Under the Abbasids, the new Islamic capital of Baghdad became a prosperous cultural, social and commercial centre of a huge trading empire (until the Mongol conquest of Baghdad in 1258). The dynasty also witnessed a golden age of Islam, with scholarly thought revitalized, and major developments in the fields of the arts, sciences, law, medicine and literature.

Utilizing the knowledge of Greece and in particular India, Muslim mathematicians established algebra (from Arabic *al-jabr*, 'completion') as a discipline distinct from geometry and arithmetic. The Persian scholar Muhammad ibn Musa al-Khwarizmi wrote the first algebraic textbook, *The Compendious Book on Calculation by Completion and Balancing* (the title that gave us 'algebra'), in 830 CE. Latin translations of his book, which spread to Europe in the twelfth century, had a major impact on the advance of mathematics in the West. His place-value decimal system, developed from Indian sources, also introduced 'Hindu–Arabic' numerals to the Islamic world, and thereafter to Europe.

12 KNIGHTS OF THE ROUND TABLE

General turmoil and migrations of people in Europe led to the emergence of new kingdoms, among them the Frankish kingdom in France, and to the settlement of Britain by the Germanic-speaking Angles, Saxons and Jutes. In Britain, the invasions gave rise to the famous legend of King Arthur who, according to folklore and stories, led the defence of Britain against Saxon invaders in the early sixth century. (The debate continues as to whether Arthur was a real historical figure or not.)

The group of stories that make up the Arthurian legend portray Arthur as the sovereign of a knightly fellowship known as the Knights of the Round Table (this table was a symbol of the famous order of chivalry). While over a hundred knights are associated with the Arthurian legends, the Round Table's chief characters are twelve knights: Lancelot du Lac, Galahad, Perceval, Kay, Tristram, Gawain, Gareth, Lamorak, Gaheris, Mordred, Bors and Bedivere.

The Arthurian legend was first brought into European literature by Geoffrey of Monmouth's highly fictional *Historia Regum Britanniae* (1135–38). Its popularity spawned new Arthurian stories, and Arthur's twelve knights may well be interlinked to the fictional stories of the Twelve Paladins, or Twelve Peers, noble knights who assist the great Frankish emperor Charlemagne (742?– 814) in defending Christendom from Muslim Saracens and pagans from the north. The number twelve, of course, is symbolic of the twelve apostles, with the king or ruler the Jesus figure.

2-HULLED CANOE

Between around 2500–1500 BCE, the islands of the central and southern Pacific Ocean had been settled by Polynesians, a seafaring people whose ancestors may have come from Taiwan, east Asia and later South-East Asia. From around 400 CE, these skilled mariners crossed thousands of miles of open ocean to settle on the distant islands of Hawaii and Easter Island, with Polynesian people known as the Maori beginning to settle New Zealand in around 1000 CE.

Easter Island head

To navigate the seas, Polynesians developed a sophisticated system based on observing the stars and sun, flight patterns of birds, ocean waves and wind. Their primary voyaging craft was a double canoe made of two hulls bound to a central platform to which was attached a fixed sail. Using long paddles to steer, these canoes transported men, women, children, animals and all sorts of food supplies, crops and equipment hundreds if not thousands of miles (voyages reached as far as Chile), some 3,500 km (2,200 miles) east of Easter Island.

240 PENNIES

In Britain, the pre-decimal pound made up of 240 pennies, or 20 shillings (equalling 12 pence) owed its existence to the Anglo-Saxon King Offa of Mercia (757–796). He in turn based his silver pennies on the new currency system of Charlemagne's Frankish empire, which had abolished the gold standard in favour of a monetary system based on a pound of silver (*livre*, a unit of both money and weight), made up of 20 *sous* (the later shilling) and 240 *deniers* (the later penny). The system was to survive in Britain for another 1,200 years.

Charlemagne, king of the Franks (768–814), was a charismatic leader who built on the successes of his forebears, Charles Martel and Pepin the Short. He instituted a number of monetary and legal reforms, while promoting learning, culture and the arts (their revival is called the Carolingian Renaissance). From 772 he also instigated a thirty-year campaign to conquer and Christianize Europe, later ruling over a Frankish empire that encompassed France, part of Spain and Germany and much of Italy. Having rid Italy of the Lombards, he was invited to Rome by Pope Leo III and crowned Holy Roman Emperor on Christmas Day 800 CE. This inaugurated what would become the Holy Roman Empire, which as a union of central European territories, formed a driving force behind the Crusades (see pages 66–67).

3-LEAVED CLOVER

Legend has it that St Patrick, in his quest to bring Christianity to Ireland, used the shamrock (a young sprig of clover) to explain the Trinity to unbelievers. 'Is it one leaf or three? . . . and so it is with God.' (Christian doctrine defines God as three persons: the Father, the Son and the Holy Spirit.)

During the fifth century CE, St Patrick, now the patron saint of Ireland, went on to convert much of Ireland to Christianity. By the late seventh century, Christianity had spread across the British Isles and monasteries had been established in Gaul and Germany, while in Italy, St Benedict had formed a monastic community in around 500 CE. Monks acted as advisers to the Christian leaders of the Frankish empire, which further consolidated the Christian religion as it extended its borders in Europe. By 800 CE, Western Europe was ruled entirely by Christian kings, whilst missionaries, largely assigned by the Byzantine Church, focused their activities on eastern and central Europe.

29.5302 Days

One of the greatest achievements of the Mayans – a 2,000-year civilization based in what is now Yucatan (Mexico), Guatemala and Belize – is their amazingly complex calendar system. Its two calendars – one a 260-day ritual almanac, primarily used to foretell the future and avoid bad luck, and the other a remarkably accurate 365-day yearly calendar based on the orbit of the sun – shared aspects developed by earlier Mesoamerican civilizations, such as the Olmec (see page 28).

Key to the system was a detailed knowledge of astronomy, and Mayans were keen observers of the sky, mapping out the path of celestial objects, particularly Venus and the Moon. In fact, using just the naked eye, Mayan astronomers reckoned the length of the lunar cycle as 29.5302 days, just a few seconds short of the 29.53059 days calculated by modern astronomers.

Remains of many Mayan buildings have features that align to celestial events, and their round temples, in particular the

Caracol at Chichen Itza, are thought to have been built as astronomical observatories. Other Mayan remains include huge stone temples standing on pyramids – all built without the use of draft animals or carts, as Mayans had not invented the wheel. The towns and cities of the Maya date back to around 600 BCE, and during the peak of its civilization, between the fourth and eighth centuries CE, Mayan lands were divided between more than fifty city-states, with populations ranging from 5,000 to 50,000. Agriculture sustained the Mayan culture, in particular the cultivation of corn or maize in fields that were cleared from the rainforest.

From around 790 CE, many of the Mayan lowland cities went into decline, so that by 950 CE, the population, once around 2 million, dropped to just a few tens of thousands. Mayan civilization continued in a diminished form until the arrival of the conquistadors (see page 89), although today around 4 million descendants still speak the Mayan language.

Just 4 Books

Thousands of Mayan books made up of bound bark paper once existed, but most were destroyed during the Spanish conquest and only four now survive. The Mayans' complex hieroglyphic text is now largely found on stone monuments, lintels, stelae and ceramic pottery, and it is only in the last thirty years that it has been fully decoded, giving historians insight into the achievements and belief systems of the Maya.

Like many other pre-Columbian societies, the Maya worshipped the jaguar, among dozens of other gods, and human sacrifice was also integral to their worship. (Ball games also formed part of their religious worship, and ball courts, seen as the gateway to the underworld, were built in every Mayan city.) The Mayan number system was based on the number twenty and a bar symbol represented five and a dot the number one. The Mayan also independently developed the concept of zero, represented by the symbol of a shell.

600 Pyramids

On the central plateau of Mexico stood a vast city named Teotihuacan ('the place of the gods'). Carefully arranged within a grid plan, it covered some 21 square km (8 square miles) and was made up of 600 pyramids, 2,000 apartment compounds, 500 workshop areas and numerous squares. Its centre was dominated by the immense pyramids of the Moon and Sun, the latter standing at over 65 metres (210 feet) high with a base of 210 metres (690 feet). The city's central road, lined with shrines and tombs, was known as the Avenue of the Dead.

The city reached its greatest extent between 250–650 CE, both as a ceremonial religious centre and a commercial hub, controlling much of Mexico's trade in obsidian (a dark-green volcanic rock). Little is known about the city's political structure or even the 100,000 people who lived there, as no written records survive. In around 650 CE, Teotihuacan was violently destroyed for reasons as yet unknown.

1 Million Urban Dwellers in Chang'an

By the seventh century CE, with the succession of the Tang Dynasty in 618, China became the most advanced and civilized country in the world. Its capital, Chang'an (now Xi'an), was certainly the world's largest city, with an urban population of one million people – a figure that European cities like London and Paris would not reach for a thousand years.

China's urban areas, and Chang'an in particular, became cosmopolitan centres of commerce and craftsmanship, a result partly of the reopening of the lucrative Silk Road trade route (see page 43) that gave China direct access to Persia, the Middle East, India and central Asia. Using its large conscripted armies (drawn from a population of fifty million), the Tang had also conquered several neighbouring regions, giving China considerable cultural influence over South-East Asia, Tibet, Japan and Korea.

In turn, literature and the arts flourished, as did ceramic production – porcelain made its first appearance during the Tang period. While paper had already been in use in China for five centuries, woodblock printing was also introduced under the Tang, so that books were printed centuries before the rest of the world.

2,490-KM GRAND CANAL

Although Chang'an was China's biggest city, the city of Yangzhou was the economic hub of the Tang era, largely because of its proximity to the Grand Canal. This was a 2,490-km (1,550-mile) network of canals and rivers completed under the Sui dynasty between 605 and 611 CE. Linking the Yangtze delta with the northern regions around what is now Beijing, the canal carried army troops and traders, as well as salt, grain, vegetables and luxury goods, providing a vital artery for China's growing trade and economy, and for the cities that sprang up along its course.

10,000 Leaves

One of the greatest literary achievements of Japan's ancient period was the *Man'yoshu*, meaning 'Collection of Ten Thousand Leaves' (perhaps referring to its many poems or pages, or suggesting that it was a work that would last 10,000 ages). The collection of 4,500 poems was compiled at some point after 759 CE, during Japan's Nara period, although it included poetry written a century or more earlier. Its poetry is noted for its imagery and emotional power, with most of the collection made up of *tanka*, five-line short poems, a classic Japanese form still in use today.

The Nara period in Japan (710–794 CE) saw not only a flowering of poetry but also the creation of Japan's first works of literature, which offer legendary accounts of Japan's imperial beginnings. Under Empress Gemmei, Japan's capital was moved to Nara, and this was modelled closely on Chang'an, the Tang capital of China. From around the fifth century CE, China had exerted greater influence on Japan and the government of Japan was increasingly organized along Chinese lines. Buddhism, brought to Japan by Chinese monks, became Japan's official religion in 538 CE (although the ancient Japanese religion of Shinto was still practised). The cultural influence of China was felt at all levels, so that the Japanese adopted Chinese written characters and even elements of Chinese fashion (the kimono resembles the clothing of China's Tang dynasty).

100 VIKING WARRIORS

The largest Viking ship ever found, discovered by chance in 1996 in Roskilde, Denmark, is almost 36 metres (118 feet) long (4 metres longer than Henry VIII's flagship *Mary Rose*, built 500 years later). Constructed after 1025 CE, the ship's size would have enabled it to carry around a hundred Viking warriors, who were needed to power the ship's thirty-nine pairs of oars alongside the ship's square sail.

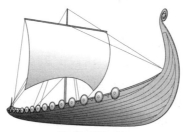

The Roskilde ship

Built possibly for King Canute, the ship probably formed part of a fleet, and would have covered the water at a top speed of 20 knots. Viking fleets could number hundreds of ships, so that great armies of warriors, perhaps as many as 10,000 men, could suddenly land and attack coastal areas with ruthless efficiency.

By this means, the Vikings from the eighth to eleventh centuries sailed from their Scandinavian homeland to raid, trade and settle in wide areas across the coasts of Europe and beyond. Their wooden longships, with long, shallow hulls, were able to sail long distances across rough seas or on shallower river waters, the ships pointed at each end so they could move forward or backwards without turning round.

Successive Viking raids on the British coast in the ninth century led to Viking settlements around Dublin and northern

England (the Danelaw). King Canute ruled England from 1016 until 1035, uniting the crowns of England and Denmark. Elsewhere, the Vikings reached Constantinople and the Middle East by sailing down the rivers of western Russia. Sailing westward, they also made the first known voyages to Iceland, Greenland and the North American continent: Leif Ericsson reached Newfoundland (now in Canada) in the eleventh century.

10,000 Norman Soldiers

The Viking descendants of northern France, the Normans, were later to invade England under their leader William, Duke of Normandy. With an assembled army of 4,000–7,000 soldiers, William defeated the Anglo-Saxon King Harold II at the Battle of Hastings, and was crowned William I, King of England, at Westminster Abbey on Christmas Day 1066.

Once England had been conquered, the Normans, now numbering, even with later recruits, just 10,000, went on to subdue England's population of 1.5 million. William did this by replacing Anglo-Saxon leaders in government, the Church and elsewhere with Norman lords and knights, seizing the land of any Saxon who had fought against him and distributing it among his Norman followers. On these lands and on his own Crown lands, he built an impressive number of fortified stone castles (pre-Norman England had not one stone building).

In return for land, each landholder or lord had to swear loyalty to the king. These tenants-in-chief (including churchmen) owed the king military service or cash payment in lieu of this, and leased land to lesser nobles who also in return paid military or financial payments. The peasant tenants, made up of free and unfree peasants, included villeins (about 40 per cent of the population) who owned property but had to work on their lord's land for two to three days a week. At the bottom of the heap were the serfs (around 10 per cent of the population), who had no property rights and could be bought and sold by the lord. This was the basis of feudalism, an economic and political system that held sway over much of Europe in the Middle Ages.

120 ACRES

In 1085, William I commissioned a survey, later to be known as the Domesday Book, to discover the resources and taxable values of all the boroughs and manors of England. Taxable land was based on 'hides' – a hide represented the amount of land that could support a household, varying from 60–120 acres (24–49 hectares). The Domesday Book provides a snapshot of life in England in around 1086, revealing that the king and his family held around 17 per cent of the land, bishops and abbots 26 per cent, and around 190 lay tenants held about 54 per cent (and of these, twelve or so leading barons controlled almost a quarter of the total land in England).

26 MILLION STRINGS OF CASH COINS

Many of China's – and the world's – most significant technological advances under the Song Dynasty (960–1279). A surge in population (it doubled between the tenth and eleventh centuries), along with a monetized economy and a spread of literature and knowledge aided by the invention of woodblock printing, led to impressive advances in technology, science, philosophy and mathematics.

Paper banknotes were first issued by the Chinese government of the Song Dynasty. Before the use of paper, the Chinese minted coins with holes in the middle so they could be strung on rope. In 960, with too little copper to strike its coins, the Song issued the first banknotes (known as *jiaozi*), and by the early twelfth century the amount of banknotes issued in one year amounted to an annual rate of 26 million strings of cash coins.

Chinese innovations also include the world's first mechanical clock, created in 1086, and the eleventh-century invention of printing using moveable type – individual pieces of type that can be rearranged and reused to print different texts – usually attributed to fifteenth-century Germany. The earliest known written formula for gunpowder dates from China in 1044 and the development of the projectile-fire cannon and gun barrel date to late Song China in the thirteenth century. The Chinese had also been smelting iron ore since 200 BCE, and in 1078 CE their iron production levels were still higher than those achieved in Britain in 1788.

9 CRUSADES

A crusader

The Crusades (from the Latin word *crux*, 'cross', displayed in blood-red on the tunics of Crusaders) were a series of military clashes fought between European Christians and Muslims over the control of the Holy Land, Palestine. Two hundred years of conflict, from 1095 to 1291, achieved little for the Christians of Europe, as most of Palestine remained in Muslim hands. However, trade and travel flourished between the two worlds, as exotic Middle Eastern foods, textiles and other goods made their first appearance in Europe. Arab innovations and ideas, such as Hindu–Arabic numerals and algebra, were also passed on, and helped enhance Europe's Renaissance.

The Crusades are commonly divided into nine major crusades (some historians list only seven or eight), alongside numerous minor campaigns. Here are the nine crusades in brief:

The First Crusade – proclaimed in 1095, fighting began in 1096, led by the Normans. A crusader army captured Jerusalem in 1099, having massacred its Muslim inhabitants.

The Second Crusade – launched by German and French rulers in 1144 after Edessa had been taken by the Turks. This was largely a failure and ended in 1155.

The Third Crusade – after almost a century of Christian occupation, the Muslim ruler Saladin recaptured Jerusalem in 1187, prompting the third crusade (1189–92), this time led by Philip II of France, Richard I (the Lionheart) of England and Frederick Barbarossa of Germany. They took Acre but could not take Jerusalem, although Richard negotiated a truce with Saladin permitting merchants and unarmed pilgrims into Jerusalem.

The Fourth Crusade – beginning in 1202, Venetian commercial interests led to crusaders sacking Constantinople in 1203 and looting it in 1204 against the wishes of the Pope.

The Fifth Crusade – began in 1217, crusaders captured and then lost the Egyptian port of Damietta in 1221.

The Sixth Crusade – began in 1228–9. Jerusalem was recovered briefly, but was lost again in 1244.

The Seventh Crusade – beginning in 1248, the crusaders, led by Louis IX of France, tried to take Egypt in 1249, but Louis IX was taken prisoner and paid a hefty ransom.

The Eighth Crusade – fought in 1270, again by Louis IX of France, whose death from plague shortly after he landed in North Africa ended the crusade.

The Ninth Crusade – led by Prince Edward of England, 1271–2. The fall of Acre, the last remaining Christian fortress, marked the end of the crusaders' ambitions.

150,000-MARK RANSOM

On his way home from the Third Crusade, Richard I was shipwrecked near Venice in 1192 and captured by Duke Leopold of Austria, who handed him over to the Holy Roman Emperor Henry VI. The emperor demanded a colossal ransom for Richard's release: 150,000 marks (65,000 pounds of silver), which represented two to three times the annual income for the English Crown. To raise the money, the people of England were heavily taxed, and Richard was freed in 1194. (The country was impoverished for years after.) After a second coronation, Richard left for Normandy and never returned.

30 MILLION KILLED BY MONGOLS

Further east in central Asia, the Mongol conqueror Genghis Khan (meaning 'universal ruler') aimed to conquer the world. In just twenty-five years he managed to conquer more territory than the ancient Romans did in four centuries, the Mongol empire becoming the biggest land empire ever. Some historians estimate that 30 million died under the Mongols, other claim many millions more died, figures that can only be likened in scale to the Black Death (see pages 72–73) and the world wars of the twentieth century.

The Mongols were nomads from central Asia, who under the leadership of Genghis Khan captured Zhongdu (now Beijing) in 1215, before turning west and overrunning central Asia, Afghanistan and much of Persia. The Mongols fought on horseback using recurved composite bows, and won battles through a combination of utter ferocity, strategy and technology (they were the first people to use gunpowder in battle, as learned from the Chinese). Their savagery amounted to what many people have described as genocide, particularly in the cities of Persia, Afghanistan and India, where accounts speak of the annihilation of entire populations, regardless of age or gender.

By the time of Genghis's death in 1227 (when he himself said it took a year to ride from one end of the empire to the next), his successors expanded still further, conquering southern Russia and briefly invading eastern Europe. By the middle of the century, they had defeated the Song Dynasty and become rulers of China (Kublai Khan took the title of emperor in 1280). At the same time, his brother Hulagu had been further ravaging Persia and Syria, capturing Baghdad in 1258. The Mongol destruction of the irrigation system in Mesopotamia turned the region from a fertile, flourishing province to the agriculturally barren desert that it largely remains today.

The devastation wrought by the Mongols – China lost half its population, the Iranian plateau as much as three-quarters – was short-lived. By 1294, the vast empire had fractured into four separate domains, the empire finally overthrown by the Ming (see pages 74–75, 76) in 1368.

1 IN 200 MEN

American research has shown that 8 per cent of men in Asia in a region stretching from the Pacific to the Caspian Sea share a Y-chromosomal lineage with a single male living in Mongolia around 900 years ago. This equates to about 16 million individuals, 1 in 200 men living on the planet today. They concluded that the likely progenitor was Genghis

Khan, who, along with his descendants, had a great many children with wives and other women. After the Mongol empire broke up, his male descendants continued to rule large chunks of the former empire for centuries, and they too sired many children.

9 SACKS OF SEVERED EARS

After the Battle of Liegnitz, fought between the Mongol Empire and a combined European force in Poland in 1241, it is said that the Mongols cut off the right ear of each fallen European in order to count the dead, amounting to a grisly nine sacks of severed ears.

MARCO MILLIONS

The Italian merchant traveller Marco Polo was known to his fellow Venetians as Marco il Milione (Marco Millions), in possible reference to his tendency to exaggerate when describing his travels in Asia. The nickname was also used as the title for his book, *Il Milione,* a chronicle of his travels around the world, and some say a distorted and fabricated account of places that he (or at least people he knew) had visited.

Marco Polo, with his uncle and father, embarked on his epic journey to Asia in around 1271. After travelling along the Silk Road, he was apparently welcomed into China by the Mongolian emperor Kublai Khan. The Polos remained in China for sixteen or seventeen years, returning to Venice in around 1295, whereupon (after a brief spell in prison in Genoa) he astonished Europeans with tales of a great civilization in the East. His accounts, whether fabricated or not, influenced explorers in later centuries, not least Christopher Columbus (see page 87), as well as Western merchants in search of lucrative spices in the East.

13 Bronze Heads

In 1938, thirteen heads, superbly cast in bronze, were discovered in the grounds of a royal palace in Ife, Nigeria. Their beauty, realism and incredible craftsmanship astonished the art world, challenging Western conceptions of African art and civilization.

It is now thought the heads were made as late as the fifteenth century, a good few centuries after the ancient Yoruba city of Ife had grown into a substantial settlement, well connected to the trade networks of West Africa. The heads are thought to depict the Oonis (rulers) of Ife, and the current Ooni's headgear still resembles that worn by medieval predecessors.

100 Years War

Fought between England and France, the Hundred Years War in fact lasted for 116 years (1337–1453), and was not a single, continuous war, but rather a series of attempts by English kings to dominate France.

Ever since 1066, England had controlled a large amount of land in France, which led to friction between the two nations. The trigger for the Hundred Years War was the confiscation of Aquitaine in 1337 by Philip IV of France, causing Edward III of England to claim the French Crown. At the outset, the English were victorious, Edward defeating Philip at Crécy in 1346, when English archers used the superior weapon of the longbow to lethal effect against armoured knights.

A decade-long break in fighting after the outbreak of the Black Death in 1347 (see below) led to several defeats for Edward, and by the time of his death in 1377 only Calais, Bordeaux and Bayonne remained under English rule. In 1415, England's Henry V renewed the English claim to the French throne, defeating the French at the Battle of Agincourt. After Henry's death in 1422, the English under the Duke of Bedford had several successes until 1429, when Joan of Arc, 'the maid of Orleans', helped the French forces break the English siege at Orleans. The French gradually won back their territories, fired by patriotism after Joan had been burnt at the stake, until in 1453 England retained only Calais and the Channel Islands.

25 MILLION DEATHS IN EUROPE

During the fourteenth century a particularly virulent form of the bubonic and pneumonic plague swept through Asia, Europe and the Middle East, resulting in an estimated 25 million deaths in Europe (on average a third of the population), another 25 million or more in Asia and unknown millions in the Middle East. Death rates varied hugely between regions, with some areas left untouched, whereas in others whole villages, communities and families were wiped out. In Europe, the population did not reach its pre-1348 level until the early sixteenth century.

The plague's origins are uncertain, but it is thought it first arose in China in the 1330s, before rapidly travelling west along the Silk Road, carried by Mongol armies, merchants and other travellers. It spread particularly fast via sea routes, carried by the fleas infesting the rats that swarmed on ships. The Black

Death first reached Europe in 1347, and caused havoc in the Byzantine Empire. In Constantinople it was known as the 'Great Dying'. Soon it assaulted European cities, including Venice, where by March 1348, around 600 a day were dying (an eventual three-fifths of all Venetians). By 1351, the disease had spread to most of Europe (though Poland, Belgium, part of south-west France and eastern Germany remained unaffected) as well as various parts of the Middle East, including Egypt, Lebanon, Syria, Iraq, Persia and Turkey.

This catastrophic toll on populations caused drastic changes in the society and economy of affected regions. In Western Europe in particular, a shortage of labour increased the bargaining power of the peasantry, and offered a chance to break free of their virtual enslavement to their masters or the king. As a result, uprisings among workers grew in number and included the *Jacquerie* revolt in 1358, a peasant uprising staged north of Paris in France, and the rebellion of English peasants in 1381, led by Wat Tyler against King Richard II's new poll tax.

2–7 DAYS

Most people infected by the plague died within two to seven days. First signs included black swellings or hard pus-filled boils appearing first on the armpits, groin and neck, followed by acute fever and vomiting of blood. There was no cure or preventative treatment except to steer clear of those infected by this terrifying disease.

12,000 SLAVES IN SILK

In 1324, Mansa Musa, the emperor of the West African empire of Mali, set out on a pilgrimage to Mecca from his capital Niani. With him came 60,000 men, 12,000 slaves dressed in Persian silk and brocade, 80 camels each carrying 136 kg (300 pounds) of gold, and another 500 slaves carrying gold staffs.

The people of Cairo, who received the emperor and his dazzling procession, were stunned by his spectacular wealth. It is said that he flooded the Cairo market with so much gold that its value declined and was not to recover for more than a decade.

During his pilgrimage, one of Mansa Musa's generals conquered the Songhai capital of Gao, expanding the vast Mali empire that at its peak (around 1350) occupied the whole of the Senegal Basin, running about 1,600 km (1,000 miles) inland. It ruled over 400 cities, and only the Mongol Empire at the time was bigger. Musa's great wealth stemmed from Mali's control of the lucrative caravan trade of the Sahara (including the great trading centre of Timbuktu), along with three huge gold mines in the south (which provided half of the Old World's supply of gold).

1 MILLION PIECES OF POTTERY A YEAR

By the early fifteenth century, China was streets ahead of Europe in terms of wealth, production and sophistication. By 1420, the Ming capital of Nanjing was the largest city in the world, with a population of around 500,000 to 1 million people. (London's population, at 40,000 and still damaged by the ravages of the Black Death and other epidemics, was not even a tenth of Nanjing's.) Nanjing also had a prosperous silk and cotton industry, and produced a million pieces of fine pottery a year, mostly for export.

In 1421, the Emperor Yongle (the name means perpetual happiness) moved the Chinese capital to Peking (Beijing) after he had constructed the Forbidden City (Gugong) as the seat of the Ming Dynasty. Made up of nearly one thousand buildings, it took more than 1 million workers fourteen years to build the Forbidden City, using wood, marble and other materials found across the empire of China.

1.4 Million Square km

By the fifteenth century, the West African state of Songhai had rebelled against the Mali empire and established their own state, seizing much of Mali's territory, securing several key trade routes and cities, and the still lucrative trade in gold. By the 1500s, under the Askia dynasty, the Songhai Empire covered around 1.4 million square km (540,000 square miles), Africa's largest empire to date.

63 Ships and 28,000 Sailors

In 1413, a Chinese fleet comprising sixty-three ships and 28,000 sailors reached the Swahili east coast of Africa. At the end of the same century, Europe's most celebrated explorer Vasco da Gama had only four ships and 500 sailors when he entered the Indian Ocean in search of a maritime route to the Spice Isles' golden lure.

At the helm of China's huge fleet of ships was court eunuch and commander Admiral Zheng He. Between 1405 and 1424, Zheng, sponsored by the Ming dynasty's Emperor Yongle, embarked on seven epic voyages, sailing to Brunei, Thailand, India, South-East Asia, Arabia and the Horn of Africa.

His fleet consisted of 300 ocean-going junks, his colossal treasure ships much larger than any built in Europe at the time. One full-size replica of a treasure ship of Admiral Zheng is, at 122 metres (400 feet) long, almost five times the size of the *Santa Maria*, the largest of the three ships that carried Christopher Columbus on his 1492 voyage across the Atlantic.

These huge fleets and navy – bigger than anything seen in the West until the First World War – accompanied a standing army of around a million troops. The Ming dynasty, which had ruled over China since 1368, had established political unity and a stable government, resulting in a flourishing industry, improvements in farming, and a doubling of the population during the first two centuries of Ming rule. Zheng's voyages were designed to display the power and wealth of Ming China, although by the early fifteenth century, maritime expeditions came to end when the Ming Dynasty, in a bid to isolate themselves from foreign influence, forbade any kind of sea voyage.

12 MILLION UNDER THE INCAS

As the Ming secured control in China, the Inca in South America were amassing a vast empire that by 1500 numbered some 12 million people. The ruling dynasty of the Inca was established in around the twelfth century from their capital Cuzco in Peru. From the early fifteenth century, over a period of a hundred years, a series of conquests led by Pachacuti Inca Yupanqui (1438–71) and his successors expanded the Inca empire to ten times its original size, so that it took in northern Ecuador, Peru and Bolivia and, from around 1529, parts of northern Argentina and Chile.

To enable this growth, Inca rulers developed a strict and effective form of centralized government upheld by a highly stratified social system. A vast network of roads, where couriers and runners relayed messages between government officials, snaked along the Pacific coast and inland along the Andes – amounting to around 25,000 km (15,500 miles) of roads, second only in size at the time to the road network of the Roman Empire. Inca technology and architecture was highly developed, with workshops and factories producing metal artefacts, textiles and ceramics. Hillside terraces produced the crops – such as maize, tomatoes, peanuts and cotton – that fed the economy of the Inca, while its religion centred on the official state cult of the sun-god Init.

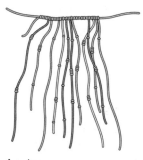

A *quipu*

48 Cords

Lacking a writing system, the Inca developed a string-and-knot device called a *quipu*, which stored information and lists. It consisted of a long rope from which hung forty-eight secondary cords and various tertiary cords. The cords were coloured differently to designate different issues of government – such as tax obligations, military numbers or information relating to ceremonial calendars. Knots made in the carefully positioned cords represented units, tens and hundreds.

20 MILES A DAY

The primary transportation system for the Inca empire, much of it forbiddingly mountainous, was the fleecy pack animal, the llama. (For an empire that did not use the wheel, the llama played a crucial role in its operations, so much so that llama figurines were often buried with the Inca dead as offerings to the gods.) As the Inca expanded down the Andes, they bred thousands and thousands of llamas that could carry all sorts of produce along its vast network of roads at high altitudes and in cold temperatures, covering around 32 km (20 miles) a day. They also provided manure for fertilizer and fuel, wool for textiles, as well as meat for food and hides for leather after their deaths. When the Spanish invaded (see page 89) not only did their guns and armour supersede the Inca technology, but their horses swiftly replaced the llama as Spanish America's main beast of burden.

20,000 SACRIFICIAL DEATHS

In 1487, at the reconsecration of the Great Pyramid of Tenochtitlan (where Mexico City now stands), Aztec priests sacrificed some 20,000 people over the course of four days. On four stone tables sited at the top of the temple, it is presumed that victims were laid before having their abdomens sliced open, their hearts ripped out, and their bodies jettisoned over the sides of the temple. Some estimates put the number of those sacrificed at over 80,000, and the ritual was not uncommon within Aztec society.

Religion dominated the Aztecs, much of it attuned to their solar calendar (adopted from the Maya – see page 57). To prevent the imminent destruction of the world, the Aztecs believed they needed to appease the gods, in particular the sun god Huitzilopochtli. He needed to be fed human hearts and blood so as not to wreak his anger on the Aztec people. For this reason, the Aztec frequently performed elaborate rituals involving human sacrifices, often of prisoners captured in war, a practice that so horrified the Spanish conquistadores that they subsequently destroyed many of the Aztec temples.

The need to provide their gods with more and more sacrificial victims drove the Aztecs to conquer their neighbouring lands, so that by 1500 the main Aztec city of Tenochtitlan ruled over an empire consisting of more than 10 million citizens living within 400–500 small states. Compulsory levies, in the form of gold or slaves, were extracted from conquered people, and goods like turquoise, resin and shells were traded across the region. The wealth generated enabled the Aztecs to build extensive roads and canals, and splendid pyramids and palaces. Tenochtitlan grew into one of the biggest cities in the world at the time, around five times the size of Tudor London.

10 Gurus and 5 Ks

The monotheistic religion of Sikhism was founded in the Punjab area of India during the fifteenth century. It combined elements of Hinduism and Islam, accepting the Hindu concept of karma and reincarnation but rejecting the caste system. Followers of Sikhism consider themselves disciples of the founder Guru Nanak ('guru' means teacher, 'sikh' means disciple) and his nine successors. Nanak died in 1539 and Sikhs believe the subsequent nine gurus were inhabited by a single spirit. The tenth and last guru, Gobind Singh (born 1666, guru 1675–1708), founded in

1699 a brotherhood of warriors known as the Khalsa, in response to their persecution by Mughal rulers.

The ceremony to join the Khalsa is now an important rite of passage in Sikhism, and its followers are required to wear the outward emblems known as the Five Ks, which are *kes* (uncut hair and beard, worn in a turban), *kangha* (comb to hold the topknot in place), *kirpan* (sword or knife), *kara* (steel bracelet) and *kachh* (shorts). Baptized male Sikhs take the name Singh (meaning 'lion') and females today take the name 'Kaur' ('princess').

3 YEARS TO MAKE THE GUTENBERG BIBLE

In 1450, the German metal-worker Johannes Gutenberg was producing printed material using a new printing press. Known as moveable type, it utilized a system of casting individual metal letters that could be arranged in rows of words and reused. This system, which Gutenberg had been developing for a number of years, speeded up the printing of books without sacrificing quality, displacing earlier methods of printing invented by the Koreans and Chinese as far back as the ninth century.

Gutenberg's first major printed book was the Gutenberg

A page from the Gutenberg Bible

Bible, a German translation of the Latin Vulgate, completed in 1455. Each book had 1,282 pages and the casting of the metal type took six months. It took another two years to set and print it – a total of three years in production – the time it took a scribe to write the Bible out in longhand. But Gutenberg's Bible had a print run of 180 copies, a huge gamble for which he had to raise money all across Europe. Illuminated decoration would then be added by hand, its extent dictated by how much each buyer could pay. The style of type used resembled contemporary handwriting and, with its strong horizontal and vertical lines, gave the impression of a woven cloth or textile (hence the word 'text').

Gutenberg's gamble paid off. Soon Germany was awash with printing presses, as was the rest of Europe, with printers in some 270 European cities by the end of the fifteenth century. This amounts to the printing of between 15 and 20 million publications, rising tenfold by the end of the following century.

The book, once a rare, mysterious work of art, the privilege of the few, became a tool and chattel of the many. This new technology had a radical effect: it speeded the flow of ideas and information across borders, bolstered the Protestant Reformation (see page 83), the Renaissance (see pages 82–83), the sharp rise in literacy, and the spread of European vernacular, and gave a new impetus to the diffusion of technology.

HEAD ⅛ OF A MAN'S HEIGHT

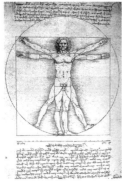

The *Vitruvian Man*

In around 1490, the Florentine artist, engineer and master of numerous other disciplines, Leonardo da Vinci, created the drawing known as the *Vitruvian Man*. Showing a man in two superimposed positions, set within a circle and square, the drawing demonstrates the ideal proportions of the human body based on those described by the ancient Roman architect Vitruvius in *De architectura*. Accompanying text shows that each part of the body is in direct proportion to the other: the length of the outspread arms is equal to a man's height, the foot is one-seventh of a man's height and the head (from the chin to the top of the head) is one-eighth the height of man.

By imposing the principles of geometry on the configuration of a human body, Da Vinci believed the workings of the body to be an analogy of the workings of the universe. This blending of art and science, drawing on the principles of Antiquity, epitomizes the new thinking of the Renaissance – an artistic and intellectual 'rebirth' that first emerged in Italy in the fourteenth and fifteenth centuries, later spreading to the rest of Europe. This reawakening of thought and learning was largely stimulated by the recovery and study of texts from Ancient Greece and Rome, many of which came to Europe as a result of increased contact with the Far East and Muslim worlds.

Artists like Botticelli and Michelangelo began to represent the human form with greater realism, and architects like Brunelleschi and Palladio created buildings that could be compared with the finest examples of the ancient world. Leonardo da Vinci, renowned artist (probably best known for the *Mona Lisa*), sculptor, pioneer of human anatomy, inventor, architect and engineer, epitomized the Renaissance humanist ideal, a man whose artistic talent, scientific inquiry and mechanical inventiveness were centuries ahead of their time.

95 Theses

The Protestant Reformation in Europe is said to have begun in 1517 when the Augustinian monk and professor Martin Luther nailed a list of ninety-five theses (or propositions) to a church door in Wittenberg, Germany. Luther's theses were a protest against the corruption and excesses of the Roman Catholic Church, prompted by Pope Leo X's selling of indulgences for sins to help finance the building of St Peter's Basilica in Rome.

Like many, Luther had also been influenced by the humanist writings of the Dutch scholar Erasmus, who had similarly criticised the abuses of the Church. Luther went on to translate the Bible into German and attack the central Catholic doctrines of transubstantiation (the conversion of the Eucharist into the body and blood of Christ), clerical celibacy and papal supremacy.

Luther's new ideas were translated into German and, aided by Gutenberg's printing presses, swept through Germany and then Europe, where they struck a chord with those who were already dissatisfied with Rome. By 1530, Sweden, Denmark and parts of Germany had broken with the Catholic Church, and England under Henry VIII followed suit in 1534. A form of Protestantism known as Calvinism, named after the reformer John Calvin, took root in Switzerland from the 1550s, spreading to western Germany, France, the Netherlands and Scotland.

6 WIVES OF HENRY VIII

Henry VIII of England broke ties with the Roman Catholic Church more for political convenience than religious zeal. By 1526, his seventeen-year marriage to Catherine of Aragon had produced a daughter (the future Mary I) but still no male heir.

Keen to secure the legitimacy of the Tudor claim to the Crown (and already infatuated with his courtier Anne Boleyn), Henry sought an annulment to the marriage, claiming that it had been blighted by Catherine's previous marriage to his deceased brother Arthur. The Pope refused, and crisis ensued, culminating with the Act of Supremacy in 1534, which severed the English Church from Rome and made Henry its Supreme Head.

Henry pressed on with his divorce from Catherine and secretly married Anne Boleyn, who bore him a daughter (the future Elizabeth I) but still no son. He had Anne executed on charges of adultery, and thereafter he married another four times, producing just one male heir in 1537 (the future Edward VI, who died in 1553 aged just fifteen). Henry's six wives, and their years as queen, were: Catherine of Aragon (1509–33); Anne Boleyn (1533–6); Jane Seymour (1536–7); Anne of Cleves (January 1540–July 1540); Catherine Howard (1540–2); Catherine Parr (1543–7).

150,000 TUGHRA

Suleiman the Magnificent took control of the already mighty Ottoman Empire in 1520. Constantinople had been taken by the Ottoman Turks in 1453 and renamed as the new Islamic capital Istanbul. Subsequent Ottoman conquests had expanded the empire into Palestine, Greece, Egypt, Syria and part of Safavid Persia.

Building on the wealth and political power already amassed by his predecessors, Suleiman was to expand the empire to its greatest extent, spanning three continents across 1.6 million square km (1 million square miles). In 1526, he incorporated two-thirds of Hungary into the empire, and with the help of a strong naval fleet and the North African admiral Khayr ad Din (known as Barbarossa – 'red beard'), Suleiman went on to dominate the eastern Mediterranean.

To govern so large an empire, the Ottomans needed a strong central administration, and Suleiman took pains to reconstruct the legal system (in the East, he is known as Suleiman Kanuni, 'the law maker'). He introduced major changes relating to education, taxation and criminal law, and issued a single legal code that was to last for more than 300 years. Himself a distinguished poet, Suleiman was also a great patron of the arts, overseeing the 'Golden Age' of the Ottoman Empire's architectural, artistic and literary achievements.

To communicate with officials and ambassadors across Ottoman-owned lands, Suleiman issued in the region of 150,000 'tughra' – monogrammed royal seals that were affixed to all official documents and correspondence.

The official seal of Suleiman the Magnificent

Beautifully decorated, the tughra were created by official calligraphers who staffed the Turkish chancery, the 'Divan' (the source of 'Divani', the official script of the Ottoman Empire). While these were works of art, their intricate script also prevented any kind of amendment to the text or forgery.

2,500 PER CENT PROFIT IN CLOVES

In 1519, the Portuguese explorer Ferdinand Magellan (sailing under a Spanish flag) set off in five ships in a bid to find a western sea route to the East Indies. Since around 1453, the expanding Ottoman Empire had taken over the control of the lucrative mainland spice route into Europe, forcing European traders to seek alternative sea routes to Asia (thus triggering the Age of Discovery). Magellan rounded the continent of South America, becoming the first European to navigate the Pacific Ocean, and reached the Philippines in 1521 with three ships remaining.

The vast expanse of the Pacific, however (twice the size of the Atlantic), proved fatal for much of Magellan's crew – forced to sail for over three months without fresh food or water. As a result, 242 men out of a crew of 260 died during the voyage. Magellan himself was killed in a skirmish in the Philippines. The eighteen survivors, however, captained by Juan Sebastián del Cano, made a fortune from the goods they picked up in the Spice Islands (Maluku Islands in Indonesia), in particular the 24,040 kg (53,000 pounds) of cloves they acquired, which they sold in Europe for a 2,500 per cent profit. In their one remaining ship, they sailed back to Spain around Africa, thereby completing the first circumnavigation of the globe.

Miscalculation of 15,500 km

Before Magellan, the Spanish had sent out many ships to explore the seas (chiefly in a bid to find a direct sea route to Asia), most notably with the Genoese explorer Christopher Columbus. Columbus led four voyages across the Atlantic Ocean, reaching the Americas first in 1492 – the first proof to Europe that the New World existed.

Columbus had aimed to sail to Asia, but badly misjudged its distance, thinking that Japan was 3,862 km (2,400 miles) away when in fact it is more than 19,312 km (12,000 miles) from Spain. Instead of reaching Asia, he came across the islands of the Caribbean, which he named the West Indies, and on Cuba (which he thought was China) he discovered tobacco. On subsequent voyages he returned to the Caribbean islands, leaving the colony he founded on Hispaniola (now divided into Haiti and the Dominican Republic) seething in rebellion. During his third voyage, from 1498 to 1500, he explored a stretch of the north-eastern shore of South America, planting a flag in what is now Venezuela. Still ranked today as one of our greatest explorers, Columbus spent his later years refusing to accept that he had not reached Asia.

The first European to reach Asia by sea was the Portuguese explorer Vasco da Gama. His four ships (dwarfed by the Chinese treasure ships of Zhang He – see pages 75–76) left Lisbon in 1497 and rounded the coast of Africa, arriving in Calicut, India, in May the following year. Only two ships made it back to Lisbon, but the cargo they carried – including the spices pepper and cinnamon – were sold at an enormous profit (worth sixty times the cost of the expedition).

The opening up of the direct sea route to Asia would prove to be hugely profitable for Portugal, prompting it to establish a vast network of ports and trading posts along the west coast of Africa, Arabia, Goa in India, the Spice Islands and Macau in China.

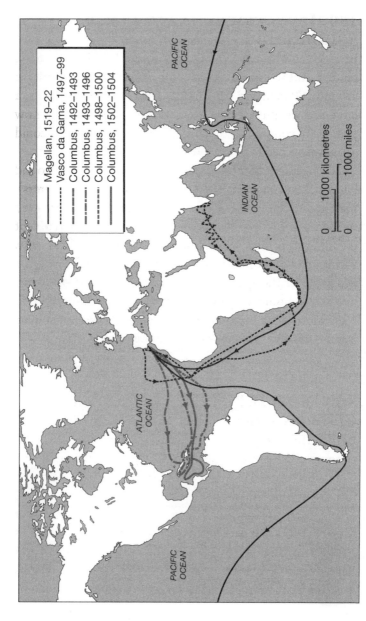

Oceanic exploration in the late 1400s and early 1500s

180 Men Conquer an Empire of 5–10 Million

In 1531, an obscure Spanish adventurer, Francisco Pizarro, landed on the coast of the Inca Empire (now Peru) with around 180 men and forty horses. He had heard stories of a large and wealthy empire in South America, which he now planned to conquer for Spain, although few believed he could actually succeed.

Having taken over the coastal settlements of Peru, Pizarro and his men, known to history as the 'conquistadors' (conquerors), marched to the Inca city of Cajamarca in 1532. There they seized the Inca emperor Atahualpa after he refused to accept the authority of the Spanish sovereign or convert to Christianity. Facing guns, cannon and horses for the first time, the Inca army fled in panic. The Spaniards slaughtered at least 7,000 of them in just two hours. In 1533, Pizarro captured Cuzco, and by 1537 most of the Inca empire and its population of between 5 and 10 million had been subdued by Spain.

Silver 15–20 Per Cent of Spanish Crown's Annual Income

Before the conquest of the Inca, the Spanish had also conquered the Aztec Empire after the Spanish official Hernan Cortes had arrived in Mexico in 1519 with an expeditionary force of around 400 men. Capturing Tenochtitlan in 1521, Spanish troops later took control of the rest of what is now Mexico, making it part of their colonial territory known as New Spain. The new Spanish territories of New Spain and Peru were to prove phenomenally profitable for Spain, as vast amounts of gold and silver were shipped to Europe, making Spain the wealthiest and most powerful country in Europe. Silver mined in Mexico and Peru not only covered the costs of running Spain's new empire but accounted for 15–20 per cent of the annual income of the Spanish Crown, with the output from silver mines rising steadily from 50 tonnes a year in the early 1500s to over 900 tonnes by 1780.

PIECES OF 8

Pieces of eight

A silver coin known as the piece of eight or Spanish dollar, worth eight *reales*, was first minted by the Spanish in the 1490s. Thanks to the vast silver deposits found in the New World, the Spanish dollar was also minted in Mexico and Peru. The coins were produced in vast numbers, and by the end of the sixteenth century a Spanish piece of eight could be spent almost anywhere in the world, from the Americas and Asia, to Africa and Europe.

About 4 cm (1.5 inches) in diameter, the Spanish dollar was the world's first global currency, and in the 1800s was still in use in South-East Asia and North America (where it was legal tender until 1857). Pieces of eight even reached Australia: a shortage of British currency in the new colony of New South Wales prompted its governor to import 40,000 Spanish dollars in 1812. A convicted forger then cut out the centres and the coins were counterstamped with 'five shillings, New South Wales'. Many of today's world currencies (including the Japanese yen, Philippine peso and US dollar) were originally based on the Spanish piece of eight.

50 Million to 5 Million

The Spanish settlers brought with them to the Americas European diseases, including smallpox, influenza, bubonic plague, cholera, typhus and a host of other diseases that killed millions, while in the silver mines or agricultural plantations, millions more were worked to death. Between 1492 and 1650, it has been estimated that the indigenous population of the Americas fell from 50 million to 5 million, a collapse of genocidal proportions.

431,286 Characters

In fifteenth- and sixteenth-century China, bureaucrats had to memorise a staggering 431,286 characters in order to pass the imperial service's gruelling examinations. Based on the Four Books and Five Classics of Confucianism, the exams were fiercely competitive, and resulted in a written language that was largely inaccessible to the great mass of people in China (in contrast to the vernacular languages of Europe, where literacy spread far more widely and quickly).

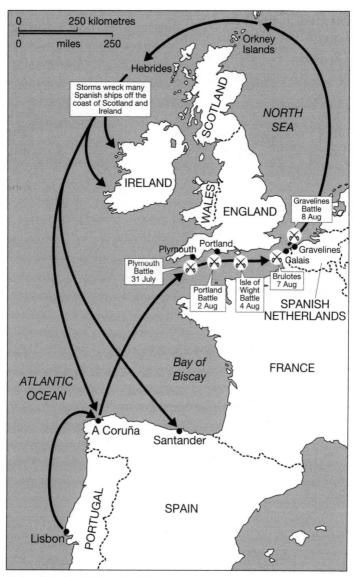

Routes of the Spanish Armada, 1588

60 Per Cent of the World's Crops From the Americas

The new era of wide-scale contact between Europe and the Americas brought not only the import of deadly diseases, but also the export of new foodstuffs and crops, as part of what became known as 'The Columbian Exchange'. Europe brought wheat, coffee and bananas, as well as cattle, horses, sheep and pigs. The Americas introduced to the world potatoes, tomatoes, squash, corn, chocolate and an abundance of other edible plants – so much so that it has been estimated that 60 per cent of all the crops grown in the world originated in the Americas.

130 Ships of the Spanish Armada

In Europe, during the sixteenth century, bitter division between the Catholic Church (still dominant in southern Europe) and the new national Protestant Churches led to a series of religiously charged wars. One of these, the Dutch Revolt – in which the northern, largely Protestant provinces of the Low Countries rebelled against the rule of the Roman Catholic King Philip II of Spain – was given support by the Protestant Queen Elizabeth I of England. In retaliation Philip, ruler of the mightiest country in Europe, planned to invade England and overthrow Elizabeth.

In 1588, the vast fleet of the Spanish Armada engaged the fleet of Elizabeth I in English waters. The ensuing battle, traditional history books tell us, led to a stunning victory for the English, who were vastly 'outnumbered and outgunned' by the Spanish fleet. In fact, out of the 130 ships that made up the Spanish Armada, only thirty-five were designed for warfare, with around nineteen of these suited to combat in stormy Atlantic waters. The Spanish had bigger, bulkier ships, but the 197 ships of the English fleet were smaller, heavily armed and more manoeuvrable.

In the end, the nimbleness of the English ships, along with the long range and rapidly reloading firepower of their cannon, brought victory. On the long retreat home, storms forced many of the Spanish Armada's ships to founder in open sea, while others were driven onto the west coast of Ireland and wrecked. Sixty ships made it back to Spain and around 15,000 men were lost at sea.

OTTOMAN ARMY OF 150,000

In 1683, a vast Ottoman army of around 150,000 laid siege to Vienna. The Viennese defenders were far outnumbered – 15,000 troops and 8,700 volunteers – but they had 370 cannons and the Ottomans just nineteen. Over a period of two months, the Turks succeeded in capturing the strong outer fortifications of the city and had begun to tunnel under, aiming to destroy the massive walls with gunpowder. When a combined Holy League army arrived, 70,000 strong and under the command of John III Sobieski of Poland, a battle fought on 12 September forced the exhausted Ottomans to retreat, having lost up to 40,000 in battle and some 20,000 during the siege. After such a crushing defeat, the Ottoman military commander Kara Mustafa was summarily executed on 25 December in the approved Ottoman manner of strangulation with a silk rope pulled by men on each end. During the rest of the century, the Ottomans lost all their European lands won by Suleiman the Magnificent. The siege of Vienna marked the end of Ottoman expansion in Europe.

5TH SAFAVID SHAH

After centuries of division, Persia had been united under the Safavid dynasty, which, from around 1500, took power and conquered Persia and parts of Iraq. The Safavids were largely responsible for bringing Shia Islam to the region, laying the foundation of an Iranian state with roughly the same boundaries as modern-day Iran.

Its fifth, and most remarkable, shah was Abbas I (reigned 1588–1629). He created a standing army and strengthened Safavid rule by expelling Ottoman and Uzbek troops from Persia. He also transformed the capital Esfahan into one of the most beautiful cities in the world, adorning it with mosques, public baths and boulevards. The city became a centre for Islamic scholarship, architecture and artistic crafts, among them the weaving of carpets, which found their way to Europe via Turkey (hence the name 'Turkish carpets'). The reign of Abbas was a period of intense commercial and diplomatic activity. Foreign ambassadors and merchants visited Esfahan and Persian diplomatic missions to Europe generated an interest in all things Persian – including the wearing of heeled shoes, a fashion that swept through Western Europe.

Abbas died in 1629 without an heir (obsessive fear of assassination had led him to either blind, execute or imprison his three sons, father and brother). The Safavid dynasty thereafter went into slow decline and was eventually conquered by Afghans in 1722 and then Nadir Shah (see pages 112–113) in 1736.

102 PASSENGERS AND 2 DOGS

In September 1620, the merchant ship *Mayflower* set sail from Plymouth, England, to North America. On board were 102 passengers (later called the Pilgrim Fathers), forty of whom were Protestant Separatists who had originally emigrated to the Netherlands to escape religious oppression and now wished to settle in the New World. The ship also carried about fifty officers and crew, and probably a few animals – the records mention two dogs (a large mastiff and a spaniel).

During the gruelling 66-day journey, two people died and one baby was born, named Oceanus Hopkins. Aiming to land in Virginia, rough seas pushed the *Mayflower* off-course, and she landed further north in Cape Cod. There they established an isolated settlement at New Plymouth in modern-day Massachusetts. Only half the settlers survived the first hard winter, but through the help of local native Americans and the ability of the Pilgrims to trade, they established the first self-contained, self-governing English community in America.

14TH CHILD

Mumtaz Mahal, the wife of the great Mughal Indian emperor Shah Jahan (reigned 1628–58), died giving birth to their fourteenth child. Driven by grief, Shah Jahan built in Agra one of the world's most beautiful structures, the Taj Mahal, in memory of his favourite of three queens (Taj Mahal is derived from her name). A blend of Indian, Persian and Islamic styles, the main buildings, including a central majestic dome reaching a height of 73 metres (240 feet), were completed in around 1638, built by more than 20,000 workers from across India, Persia, the Ottoman Empire and Europe.

15,000 in New France

The area colonized by France in North America was known as 'New France'. Beginning in 1534 when the French explorer Jacques Cartier explored the St Lawrence River, French fur traders eventually settled in Acadia in 1604, and in 1608 a trading station was established on the St Lawrence River, which grew into the city of Quebec. However, for the first few decades of the colony, the French population remained in the hundreds. The population grew when the French Crown took over the colony in 1663 and shipped over more settlers, but by 1700 the population was still just 15,000, compared with 234,000 white people in the English colonies of America.

2nd Defenestration of Prague

In May 1618, a Protestant assembly, in open revolt against the Habsburg Holy Roman Emperor Matthias and his staunchly Catholic heir Ferdinand II, threw two of the Emperor's representatives out of a castle window. They fell some 21 metres (69 feet) to the ground, and, to everyone's surprise, survived. A similar incident had been recorded some 200 years earlier in 1419 when an angry crowd of radical Czech Hussites threw fifteen members of the Prague town council out of the Town Hall window.

Both incidents provoked prolonged conflict in Bohemia, the latter famously spreading across the whole of Europe, resulting in the Thirty Years War. By 1620, Bohemian Protestant rebels had been defeated, prompting the Protestant rulers of Denmark, England and Holland to send in an invading army, which suffered several losses in Germany between 1625 and 1629. Other European powers joined in the war, among them Gustavus Adolphus, King of Sweden, who won several victories against the Catholic armies, but died in battle in 1632.

When France joined in the war on the side of the Protestants (France, under the direction of chief minister Cardinal Richelieu, was Catholic but determined to limit Habsburg power), Protestants gained the upper hand. Fighting continued and after several French victories, the war ended on 24 October 1648 when the Peace of Westphalia was signed.

The outcome of the war was that Catholic states remained Catholic while Protestant states were granted independence, and Holland soon grew into a wealthy colonial power. The population of Germany was halved by the many battles fought there. Spain lost much of its former control in Europe, and France emerged as the dominant power.

Tobacco Sold at 500–1,000 Per Cent Profit

In the seventeenth century, a string of English colonies were established on the eastern coast of North America, the first founded in 1607, in Jamestown, Virginia. Life for early colonists was perilous: 80 per cent of settlers died during the winter of 1609–10, although more settlers would later arrive, largely to work on the colony's many tobacco plantations. In Europe, there was great demand for tobacco, and the potential for huge profits for its producers. Virginian tobacco sold in London, during the 1620s, for five or ten times the amount it cost to produce in Virginia.

With an eye on further profits, the English Crown in 1632 established a new colony further north, named Maryland (in honour of Henrietta Maria, the queen consort of Charles I), which was similarly founded on the economic lure of tobacco. From their location on the vast estuary that runs inland from the Atlantic, the two colonies of Maryland and Virginia became known as the Chesapeake colonies.

100 ACRES OF LAND

For most of the seventeenth century, the inhabitants of the Chesapeake colonies were white. Many were attracted by the colony's headright system, whereby any freemen who arrived would be given a hundred acres of land. To those who had left England, where property was largely in the hands of the nobility, gentry or the Church, this seemed a generous scheme.

Most settlers – perhaps three-quarters – arrived as indentured servants. These were mostly poor, unskilled men who, after around seven years of indentured work, could work for wages or acquire the means to buy land of their own. The colonies would later import slaves (see pages 107–108) to work in the tobacco fields, a precedent set by the new colony of Carolina, founded in 1670, which was modelled on England's colony of Barbados, where slave labour was used in the production of sugar cane.

3,000 GUILDERS FOR 1 TULIP BULB

The Viceroy tulip

In 1637, a Dutch florist sold a single tulip bulb, named Viseroij (Viceroy), for 3,000 guilders, twenty times the annual salary of a skilled craftsman. A contemporary listed what 3,000 guilders would have bought at the time: 2 tons of butter, 24 tons of wheat, 454 kg (1,000 pounds) of cheese, a silver drinking cup, and even a ship – all for something that weighed less than 14 grams.

The reason for this extraordinary price was that demand for tulips, and in particular differently coloured varieties, had outstripped supply, leading to a speculative frenzy in seventeenth-century Holland known as *Tulpenwindhandel* (Tulip Mania). The craze reached its height in1633–7, when even normal middle-class families began to risk their homes and livelihood to buy tulip bulbs in the hope of larger profits at resale.

Increasingly, bulbs were sold by weight while still in the ground, buyers given only promissory notes providing details of the bulb, which were then sold on to other buyers, so that at the height of the tulip mania, trade became pure speculations. In early 1637, when doubt spread over their continued rise, prices plummeted and the tulip trade crashed, causing financial ruin for many normal Dutch families. Considered the first speculative, or economic bubble (in which asset prices are vastly inflated and likely to burst at any time), Tulip Mania compares to more recent speculative fiascos, including the South Sea bubble of 1720 and the dot-com bubble of 1997–2000.

59 Regicides of Charles I

On 27 January 1649, fifty-nine commissioners ('the regicides') signed and placed their seals on the death warrant of King Charles I. Three days later the English king was beheaded at the Palace of Whitehall, and a republic established under the leadership of Parliament's leading general, Oliver Cromwell. The commissioners who signed the death warrant – most notably Cromwell himself – were part of a group of Parliamentarians who had sat in judgement during Charles's trial. There they had convicted him of treason against England, although Charles I maintained that the trial was illegal, as no court had jurisdiction over a monarch whose authority to rule derived from God – 'the King can do no wrong'.

In 1660, when Charles's son returned to the throne of England as Charles II, the Royal Pardon, which exonerated all past treason against the Crown, specifically excluded the fifty-nine regicides. The subsequent trials led to some being publicly hanged, drawn and quartered, others imprisoned for life, and those already deceased, among them Oliver Cromwell, were exhumed and posthumously executed and mutilated, their heads displayed on poles outside Westminster Hall.

11.5 PER CENT OF POPULATION KILLED

The trial of King Charles I had followed a long armed struggle (1642–6 and 1648–9) between the Parliamentarians (known as Roundheads) and supporters of Charles I (Cavaliers). The war arose over constitutional and religious disagreements that had emerged during Charles I's autocratic 'Personal Rule' between 1629 and 1640, in which he alienated large numbers of clergy and gentry by trying to reinstate his new 'High' Anglican prayer book, among other liturgical reforms.

As a result of the two wars, plus a third period of conflict following Charles I's execution in 1649, in the period between 1642 and 1651, 866,000 people in England, Scotland and Ireland were killed. With the total population standing at 7.5 million, the death toll amounted to 11.5 per cent of the population.

60–70 PER CENT OF EDO DESTROYED

In the Japanese city of Edo (now Tokyo), a great fire broke out in March 1657, started, so legend says, by a priest who was burning a cursed kimono. Known as the Great Meireki Fire, the fire burned through the city, crossing the Sumida river and Nihonbashi canal, and spreading to the districts of Fukagawa and Kyobashi. Around 60–70 per cent of Edo was destroyed, with corpses piled high in the streets and buried in mass graves. It is estimated that 100,000 died, although it may have been as many as 200,000, half of Edo's population – comparable to the death and destruction caused by the 1923 Great Kanto earthquake and fire (150,000 were killed), and the bombing of Tokyo in 1945 (claiming over 100,000 lives).

The Tokugawa shogunate took two years to reconstruct

the city, taking the opportunity to reorganize its layout, and in particular to restore its mercantile centre. The city was the seat of power for the shogunate, whose years of rule from 1603 to the Meiji restoration in 1868 (see page 144) became known as the Edo period.

2 Centuries of Isolation

Since the mid-1500s Christian missionaries and European merchants (and in particular the technology and weaponry they brought with them) had been welcomed in Japan. During the sixteenth century, however, Christianity began to be seen as a growing threat to the stability of the shogunate, and by 1639 all missionaries and most traders were expelled. Interaction with foreign states was severely restricted and the Japanese forbidden to leave the country. This foreign policy, known as the *sakoku*, or locked-country policy, effectively remained in place for over two centuries. Cut off from global epidemics and guns, Japan enjoyed internal stability and an expanding national economy. Its population grew so fast that by 1700 Edo had become the world's biggest city.

13,200 Houses and 140 Churches Destroyed

Nine years after the fire in Edo, the Great Fire of London destroyed much of the old city of London, engulfing St Paul's Cathedral and destroying 13,200 houses and 140 churches, although just five people were killed. A previous fire of 1212 (and which prior to 1666 was also known as the Great Fire of London) killed approximately 12,000 people.

It blazed through much of Southwark and reached London Bridge (only just rebuilt following another fire in 1135), where many were trapped by fire on either side, the flames then spreading to the City of London.

45.52-CARAT BLUE DIAMOND

In 1686, the sixth Mughal emperor of India, Aurangzeb (reigned 1658–1707), set out to conquer new territories in the Indian south and the Deccan, securing most famously the world's first known diamond mine in the Golconda region. Among its gravel deposits was found the Hope Diamond (also known as the Tavernier Blue diamond), a large blue diamond weighing 45.52 carats, which was later worn by the monarchs of France. It turned up in Great Britain in the late eighteenth century, when it seems to have been recut. It now resides at the Smithsonian National Museum of Natural History in Washington DC, where it is reported to be insured for $250 million.

The conquest of the diamond mine made Aurangzeb the world's richest ruler, and under him the Mughal empire reached its greatest extent, ruling over a quarter of the world's population. But his supremacy was short-lived. A 26-year war that had started back in 1681 against the Hindu Maratha state (during which Aurangzeb is said to have travelled with a moveable city of tents and bazaars, half a million followers, 50,000 camels and 30,000 elephants) eventually stripped the land of resources, led to famine and disease, and drove his empire to the brink of bankruptcy.

Rejecting the liberalism of his Mughal predecessors, Aurangzeb also attempted to force Islam on the majority

Hindu population. He destroyed Hindu temples and shrines and alienated Sikhs by arresting and executing the ninth Sikh Guru in 1675. When he died in 1707, he left behind a hotbed of revolt, which led to the collapse of the Mughal Empire in the mid-eighteenth century.

9 Basic Rights for all Englishmen

After the Catholic James II had been deposed as English monarch in 1688 (during the Glorious Revolution) in favour of Protestant rulers William III and Mary II, Parliament in 1689 drew up a Bill of Rights, which laid down the rights of Parliament and the limits of sovereign power. This document later influenced constitutional law around the world, including the US Bill of Rights, and its influence can be seen in twentieth-century documents such as the European Convention of Human Rights and the United Nations Declaration on Human Rights.

The Act affirmed nine basic rights for all Englishmen: no royal interference with the laws; no taxation by royal prerogative; no royal interference in election of MPs; the freedom to petition the monarch without fear of retribution; no standing army without consent of Parliament; freedom of speech in Parliament; the right to bear arms for people's own protection; no validation for grants or promises of forfeitures before a trial; and no excessive or 'cruel and unusual' punishments. In a later Act of Settlement, the Bill of Rights also barred Roman Catholics from the British throne.

400,000 A Year Died of Smallpox

In Europe, the most feared disease of the seventeenth and eighteenth centuries was smallpox. Until a vaccination was discovered, it killed off more people than any other disease – 400,000 a year in Europe west of Russia – and in the eighteenth century accounted for one in ten deaths in England.

A highly contagious disease that left any survivor's face and limbs covered with cratered pockmarks, or pox, the more lethal haemorrhagic form killed 90 per cent of its victims, many of them children. Those who lived faced a lifetime of disfigurement or even blindness.

Smallpox had existed for thousands of years, endemic, for example, in parts of China in the second century CE, but it didn't become common in Europe until the early sixteenth century. It succeeded the plague as the most feared pestilence, and Europe saw frequent epidemics throughout the seventeenth and eighteenth centuries.

In 1796, an English doctor named Edward Jenner discovered a vaccine for smallpox by inoculating a healthy boy with cowpox, a mild form of the far more lethal smallpox. Vaccination programmes were instituted in many countries throughout the nineteenth century and by the beginning of the twentieth century, smallpox was no longer endemic in many countries in Europe, eradicated in the UK in 1934, USSR in 1936, the United States in 1949 and China in 1961. In 1980, the United Nations was able to announce that the disease had been entirely wiped out. Jenner's work in immunology arguably 'saved more lives than the work of any other human'.

12.4 MILLION SLAVES

An estimated 12.4 million slaves were transported from the west coast of Africa across the Atlantic to the sugar, cotton and tobacco plantations of the Caribbean, North and South America.

The slave trade usually followed a triangular system whereby ships sailed from Europe to West Africa, unloaded their manufactured goods and weaponry (used by indigenous West Africans to capture slaves) in exchange for slaves, then took the slaves to the Americas, before returning to Europe with cargoes of sugar and other colonial produce.

On their way to the New World, around 2 million died (not counting the unknown millions who died in captivity in holding pens on the African coast, or as a result of African wars in which surviving captives were marched to the coast).

During Europe's first contact with Africa, few slaves were traded, certainly no more than when the Franks, Vikings and Arab Muslims enslaved millions in the territories that they conquered during the early Middle Ages. In the main, it was the Portuguese and Spanish who began the Atlantic trade in slaves in the fifteenth century, and after them the other seafaring nations: the Dutch, English and French.

By the mid-seventeenth century, more than forty slave fortresses had been established on the west coast of Africa, by which time around 40,000 African slaves had been transported to Mexico and 30,000 to Peru. During the eighteenth century, the trade soared dramatically. In North America, slaves outnumbered free whites in South Carolina by two to one in 1740, and the tobacco plantations of Maryland and Virginia followed suit. Around 2 million slaves went to the British, French and Dutch plantations of the Caribbean during the seventeenth and eighteenth centuries, and even more – around 2.5 million between 1550 and 1800 – went to the Portuguese colony of Brazil.

AVERAGE LIFE EXPECTANCY JUST 23

Portugal had colonized Brazil in 1500 and cultivated sugar plantations there, so that by 1600 Brazil was the world's principal centre of sugar production. (Sugar cultivation – the cutting and boiling of cane – was back-breaking work and thus reserved as slave labour.) As the Brazilian economy diversified into mining and coffee-growing, slaves would continue to be used in preference to migrant labour. Conditions were generally dire, with many worked to death – as late as the 1850s the average life expectancy of a Brazilian slave was just twenty-three. Economic logic dictated that it was more cost-effective for slave-owners to replace worn-out slaves after five or six years, than to improve their conditions and encourage them to have families.

ASHANTI EMPIRE OF 3–5 MILLION

The West African Ashanti Empire made great wealth from its trade in gold, cola nuts and slaves during the eighteenth and nineteenth centuries. Slaves were sold to European trading stations established along the Gold Coast in exchange for European goods and firearms. Its territory, which covered what is now southern Ghana, Togo and the Gold Coast, had a population of 3 to 5 million, governed by a strong central administration at Kumasi. Between 1824 and 1831 and again in 1874, the Ashanti fought a series of military campaigns against the British, who were keen to establish a presence in West Africa (and who took and burned the Ashanti capital of Kumasi in 1874). Further troubles from 1895 led the British to annex the Ashanti Empire in 1901.

90 Per Cent of Russia's Gas and Coal Reserves

During the eighteenth century, Russia emerged as a major power in Europe, the vast lands of its empire stretching 12,000 km (7,500 miles) from the Baltic Sea to the Pacific Ocean. Crucially, Siberia was also under Russian control – a region extraordinarily rich in minerals, with some of the world's largest deposits of nickel, lead, diamonds, silver and zinc. (Today 90 per cent of Russia's gas and coal reserves are located in Siberia, along with 80 per cent of its oil – without Siberia, Russia would not be the energy superpower it is today.)

The previous two centuries had seen Russia grow from a small principality of Muscovy to a multi-ethnic empire. Its first Tsar Ivan IV ('the Terrible'), crowned in 1547, doubled its territory through campaigns against the Mongols and the annexation of south-western Siberia. Further territorial growth in the seventeenth century planted Russian settlements in eastern Siberia and on the Pacific coast, led mostly by Cossacks (East Slavic people mostly from Ukraine and southern Russia) hunting for furs and ivory.

Under Peter the Great, who ruled with half-brother Ivan V from 1682, and as sole ruler from 1696 to 1725, the Russian Empire rose in the world. Victory over Sweden in the Great Northern War in 1721 gave Russia access to the Baltic Sea and it went on to annex Estonia, Latvia and parts of Finland. Peter also took steps to Westernize the empire and founded a new capital on the Baltic Sea called St Petersburg (his 'window on the West').

Russian territory and influence continued to grow under Catherine the Great (ruled 1762–96). Russia came to dominate Poland and through a series of victories against the Ottoman Turks, annexed Crimea and colonized vast territories along the Black and Azov Seas.

Prussian Army of 83,000

Prussia, first proclaimed a nation in 1701, was to emerge as a major military power in the eighteenth century. Its second king, Frederick William I, devoted much of his rule to building the Prussian army into a highly efficient military machine. At the start of his reign in 1713, Prussian forces numbered 38,000 soldiers; by the time he died in 1740, the army had grown to 83,000 out of a population of 2.2 million – almost 4 per cent of the population, more than double the proportion in Austria and France.

This was achieved by gearing the whole organization of the state to war. A 'canton system' required all male peasants to serve in the military, with nobles as officers. To his son Frederick II (the Great) he bequeathed a large and well-disciplined army, along with an efficient, financially sound administration, all of which the new king used to raise Prussia's standing in Europe. In 1740, Frederick II seized the rich Austrian province of Silesia, holding on to it during the War of the Austrian Succession (1740–48) and the Seven Years War (1756–63). In the Battle of Rossbach in 1757 he defeated a combined French and Austrian army of more than 80,000 with 30,000 Prussian troops.

The Emperor's 4 Treasuries

One of China's longest-reigning emperors was Qianlong, the fourth emperor of the Qing (Manchu) dynasty, which had ruled over China since 1644. The six-decade rule of Qianlong (1735–96) took the Qing dynasty to the peak of its power, as China's territory tripled to more or less its current extent. A successful general, Qianlong destroyed Mongol power in central Asia and incorporated the vast region now known as

Xinjiang-Uighur Autonomous Region, along with Taiwan, Manchuria, Tibet and Turkestan.

On the domestic front, Qianlong championed industrial and agricultural development, which increased the wealth of the empire and boosted trade with Europe. The population grew rapidly to around 300 million people by the end of the eighteenth century.

A renowned calligrapher and poet (he published more than 40,000 compositions in his lifetime), Qianlong was also a great patron of the arts and collector of antiquities, ceramics and fine art. He particularly enjoyed sponsoring huge literary works, among them the 36,275 handwritten volumes of the *Sikuquanshu* (Complete Library of the Four Treasuries), created largely as a monument to the success of the dynasty and the prosperity of his reign. *Sikuquanshu* was an encyclopedic compilation of the main writings of 5,000 years of Chinese history; the title's 'Four Treasuries' refer to the four conventional branches of literature – classical, historical, philosophical and literary.

Beginning in 1772, it took 3,800 people fifteen years to scrutinize the texts, collate and transcribe seven copies of the *Sikuquanshu*, the largest collection of books in Chinese history. With 800 million words, it remained the largest anthology of writing in human history, only recently surpassed by the English Wikipedia, which comprises over 2.6 billion words.

250 TO 1
The Qing Dynasty was founded not by Han Chinese, who formed the vast majority of China, but by inhabitants of what is now Manchuria. In effect they were a tiny ethnic minority, outnumbered by the Han Chinese by around 250 to 1.

TWICE THE COST OF THE TAJ MAHAL
In 1739, the Persian ruler Nadir Shah (often described as the 'Napoleon of Persia') marched into Delhi, massacred about 30,000 of its inhabitants and plundered huge amounts of treasure, including the Mughals' fabled Peacock Throne and the Koh-i-Noor diamond (which eventually became part of the British crown jewels).

The Peacock Throne

The famous golden throne, known as the Peacock Throne, was originally built for the Mughal emperor Shah Jahan (see page 96). It stood on golden feet set with jewels, backed with gilded, enamelled peacock tails inset with diamonds, rubies and other stones. Wrought out of 1,150 kg (2,535 pounds) of gold and 230 kg (507 pounds) of precious stones, it cost twice as much as the Taj Mahal, also built for Shah Jahan, and in 2000 was valued in retrospect at $804 million – the costliest treasure in history.

Nadir Shah, who had seized the throne of Persia in 1736 (deposing the 200-year Safavid dynasty), had restored Persia's power through a number of military campaigns, notably against Persia's arch-rival the Ottomans. His empire briefly took in present-day Iran, Iraq, Afghanistan, Pakistan, Oman, parts of central Asia, and the Caucasus region. Nadir's Indian campaign marked the zenith of his power, after which his health declined and his rule became increasingly despotic (he blinded his own son after suspecting him of an assassination attempt).

In 1747, Shah was assassinated by one of his own guards, and his empire quickly disintegrated. In the ensuing chaos the Peacock Throne disappeared, and was probably dismantled, its stones and metals distributed elsewhere. Reproductions of the throne were made for subsequent shahs and still remain the symbol of Persian or Iranian monarchy.

45 KG OF SAUERKRAUT

During the eighteenth century, the vitamin C deficiency disease known as scurvy killed more British sailors than enemy action. So rife was the disease on all ships on long voyages, where stocks of fresh fruit and vegetables quickly ran short, that it typically killed half of all crews. Vasco da Gama (see pages 75–76, 87) lost 116 out of a crew of 170, mainly to scurvy, and Magellan (see page 86) lost 208 out of 230 – in fact an estimated 2 million sailors between 1500 and 1800 died of scurvy.

The problem was that no one knew what caused it, its symptoms so varied that it was sometimes mistaken for syphilis, dysentery or even madness. In 1753, the Scottish naval surgeon James Lind showed that the disease could be cured and prevented by eating oranges and lemons. Captain Cook was to provide the definitive evidence for this on his circumnavigation of the world in 1768–71. Rations, including 45 kg (100 pounds) of sauerkraut and lime juice, were shared among all sailors, who were also encouraged to exercise and keep themselves and their possessions clean. Not one of the crew members died during the voyage.

Within around thirty years or so, citrus fruits became common aboard ships – so much so that British sailors were nicknamed 'limeys' after the lime juice issued to them by the Royal Navy.

342 CHESTS OF TEA

The destruction of tea at Boston Harbor, 1773

On 16 December 1773, in a raid now celebrated as the Boston Tea Party, around 116 North American colonists dressed as Mohawk Indians boarded three ships in the port of Boston, hauled 342 chests of tea onto the decks, and dumped the contents overboard. Into the water went 40,800 kg (90,000 pounds) of tea worth an estimated £10,000 (around a million US dollars today). This deliberate destruction of immensely valuable cargo deprived Boston of a year's worth of tea, but would also result in revolution in the North American colonies.

The incident was the upshot of ongoing resentment between the American colonies and Britain, largely over the ever-thorny issue of taxation and the lack of colonists' representation in the British Parliament. The British government, its national debt doubled after the costly Seven Years War (1756–63), had attempted to tax the colonists on a variety of produce, which caused such an outcry that in 1770 all taxes were withdrawn, other than those on tea. This was done partly to remind the colonists of their allegiance to the Crown and also to help out the financially stricken East India Company (a British trading company that effectively monopolized tea sales in America), which had inadvertently built up vast stockpiles of tea (a whopping 7.7 million kg or 17 million pounds of it).

In response, the British closed down Boston harbour and reduced the power of local government. Armed resistance led to full-scale war in 1775 after Britain's King George III refused to compromise over taxes or listen to colonists' grievances. Public feeling swelled for independence, fuelled in part by the liberal ideals of the Enlightenment and the publication of Thomas Paine's incendiary pamphlet *Common Sense*, which argued for freedom from British rule.

With no hope of a peaceful resolution, the colonists adopted the Declaration of Independence on 4 July 1776, which unified the thirteen American colonies as 'free and independent states ... absolved from all Allegiance to the British crown'. But Britain refused to concede and the war continued for another five years. The British struggled to maintain supplies (each soldier required a third of a ton of food to be transported every year) and suffered from a lack of local knowledge and a hostile population, so that despite frequent victories, they could not destroy the armies of commander-in-chief George Washington.

It has been estimated that up to 25,000 American soldiers died in the Wars of Independence – a third on the battlefield and two-thirds from disease (and this mortality rate would have been higher had Washington not begun inoculating his troops against smallpox in 1777). Thousands of white Americans fought on the British side (about a fifth of white Americans remained loyal to the Crown) and African-Americans fought on both sides, some fearing that independence would reinforce slavery (slaves were growing in number – from around 236,000 in the US colonies in 1750 to more than a million in 1810).

The turning point came in 1778 when France joined the war on the side of the revolutionaries, followed by Spain in 1779. In 1781, a Franco-American force won the last major battle at Yorktown, Virginia, capturing over 7,000 British soldiers. The 1783 Treaty of Paris finally recognized the independence of the United States of America – while France was driven into massive debt that contributed to the outbreak of the French Revolution (see page 118).

55 DELEGATES

In 1787, fifty-five delegates devised and established the US Constitution, providing the framework for representative democracy in the US. Among the delegates, known as the 'Founding Fathers' of America, were such luminaries as George Washington, Thomas Jefferson, James Madison and Benjamin Franklin. Since its adoption, the constitution has been amended twenty-seven times.

13 Stripes

In 1777, the Continental Congress passed the Flag Resolution, which stated: '*Resolved*, That the flag of the thirteen United States be thirteen stripes, alternate red and white; that the union be thirteen stars, white in a blue field, representing a new constellation.' (The design of the new flag closely resembled that of the British East India Company.) Since then, new stars have been added on to the national flag of the US, as Americans expanded west. The last, representing Hawaii, was added in 1960, so that the flag now features fifty stars.

The 3 Estates

On Sunday 5 May 1789, the French King Louis XVI summoned for the first time in 175 years the 'Estates General', a body that represented the three 'estates' or social orders of France: the clergy, nobility, and the rest of the population, known as the Third Estate. The clergy consisted of around 10,000 people and were exempt from tax, as were the nobility, who numbered around 400,000. The Third Estate, from wealthy middle class to peasant worker, comprised approximately 25 million people, and they were required to pay taxes, although the very poorest – the farmers, peasants and workers – bore the majority of the tax burden, as many French towns had exemptions.

Financial crisis, following costly wars (in particular, aiding American rebels in the US War of Independence), had forced the French king to summon the Estates General in the hope of raising taxes. At the same time, a run of bad harvests in the 1780s had brought high food prices and crippling poverty to much of the population. (The population had swelled from 19 million in 1700 to between 24–26 million people, without any corresponding growth in food production, so if a harvest fell by as little as 10 per cent, which was common, people went hungry.)

When the Estates General convened, delegates representing the Third Estate (thus 97 per cent of the nation) complained against their lack of influence – the nobility and clergy could overrule the Third Estate. So the bourgeois leaders of the Third Estate, inspired by the liberalism of the Enlightenment and inequality in political representation, broke away and created their own convention, the National Assembly.

In Paris, the people welcomed the creation of the National Assembly and on 14 July 1789 stormed the Bastille, an old fortress and symbol of authority in Paris. Violence spread beyond Paris to rural France where 80 per cent of the population lived. In response the National Assembly abolished noble privileges, removing their exemption from tax, and ended obligations to pay tithes to the Church. They also issued the Declaration of the Rights of Man and the Citizen, a statement of principles that claimed that all men should be equal before the law and asserted man's natural right to liberty and to resist oppression, a set of principles expressed in the motto of the French Revolution: Liberty, Equality, Fraternity.

Increasing military threats led to more radical policies: the monarchy was abolished and a republic established in 1792. King Louis XVI and Queen Marie Antoinette were executed in 1793. An extreme wing of the government led by the Jacobins and their leader Maximilien Robespierre now rose to power and unleashed a reign of terror in which around 45,000 people were executed. The Terror ended after Robespierre himself was executed in 1794, after which the Directory assumed control of the French state until the Corsican general Napoleon Bonaparte seized power in 1799.

Year 1 – 1792

In a bid to remove all religious and royalist influence from the calendar and introduce decimalization in France, the French revolutionaries introduced a new calendar, which had twelve months, each with thirty days exactly. Weeks consisted of ten days, each ending with a day of rest, and days were ten hours long, hours one hundred minutes, and minutes one hundred seconds (although the week and hour reforms were largely confined to Paris).

The naming of the months – as advised by the poet-journalist Fabre d'Eglantine – was inspired by nature, and the prevailing weather of France: *vendémiaire* (grape harvest), *brumaire* (fog), *frimaire* (frost), *nivôse* (snowy), *pluviôse* (rainy), *ventôse* (windy), *germinal* (germination), *floréal* (flower), *prairial* (pasture), *messidor* (harvest), *thermidor* (heat) and *fructidor* (fruit). (Satirists in Britain ridiculed the calendar, coming up with their own nicknames for the four seasons for France: Wheezy, Sneezy and Freezy; Slippy, Drippy and Nippy; Showery, Flowery and Bowery; Wheaty, Heaty and Sweety.) Its first day started the day after the abolition of the monarchy, on 22 September, with a new count for the years – year 1 was 1792. It was used by the French government for twelve years.

4 kg of Wool

In the eighteenth century, Britain saw the stirrings of a very different kind of upheaval, a revolution in agriculture that would spur population growth and bring about enormous social and economic change.

Between around 1750 and 1850, Britain saw unprecedented growth in agricultural output, largely as a result of new techniques in farming. New breeding methods produced bigger and better animals, so that beef cattle and sheep doubled in weight between 1700 and 1800. Selective breeding also improved productivity – a typical eighteenth-century sheep yielded around 4 kg (9 pounds) of wool, six times as much as the average medieval sheep.

Other innovations included the enclosure of a quarter of Britain's farmland (formerly made up of strips in open fields) into larger, more productive plots; the adoption of Jethro Tull's seed drill, a mechanical seeder that resulted in a much better rate of germination; and a switch to a four-field crop rotation system that greatly increased crops and livestock yields, and improved soil fertility.

SPINNING 1,000 THREADS OF COTTON

The boost in agricultural output in Britain helped to fuel the transformation in manufacturing known as the Industrial Revolution. Key to this was mechanizing the cotton industry, which in the 1700s accounted for around one tenth of Britain's national income.

For centuries, the spinning and weaving of cloth was done by hand in people's homes (the 'cottage industry') until new machinery greatly boosted the speed of spinning and weaving. One such invention was James Hargreaves's 'Spinning Jenny', patented in 1770, a spinning wheel that enabled the operator to spin eight threads at once. Ten years later, Samuel Crompton's spinning mule, powered by steam or water power, could spin a thousand threads at a time.

To house these new machines, enterprising businessmen set up factories, while ironworks and coal mines sprang up to produce the raw materials to make and power the new machines. Steam-driven engines, as improved and developed by the Scottish engineer James Watt in 1782, powered many of Britain's mines, mills and factories. From the early nineteenth century onwards, steam engines would also power locomotives, and by 1855 thousands of kilometres of railway snaked across the country.

Average Life Expectancy 18.5 Years

Industrialization was accompanied by mass urbanization as workers moved from rural areas to the towns that grew around factories and mines. By 1850, half of Britain's population lived in cities. But industrialization did not bring better working conditions for many of those whom it wrenched from the seasonal rhythm of the cottage industry into the often grim conditions of the factory. Some estimates give the average number of work days a year in Britain as rising from 250 (roughly today's average) to 350 during the 1700s. (It had been quite a lot fewer than 250 days for farm workers in the Middle Ages.)

Child labour was common, although factory reforms later improved working conditions and legislated against the use of child labour. In many of the fast-growing cities, cramped, squalid housing conditions led to the outbreak of disease, notably cholera and typhus, and a desperately low life expectancy among the urban poor. The average life expectancy of a worker in Dudley in the mid-eighteenth century was just 18.5, a life-span lower than that of many African slaves and not seen in Britain since the Bronze Age.

778 CONVICTS

On the eastern shores of Australia in 1788, a fleet of eleven ships arrived. They contained around 778 British convicts, along with 443 seamen, and 211 marines, officials and their families. Landing first at Botany Bay, the fleet moved on to a more suitable natural harbour, which they named Sydney Cove, officially starting the settlement of Australia on 26 January 1788.

Eighteen years before, the British explorer Captain James Cook had landed at Botany Bay, he and his men becoming the first Europeans to reach the east coast of Australia. (The Dutch had charted the western and northern coast in the seventeenth century but had not settled there.) Thereafter, Cook claimed the whole eastern coast of Australia for Britain, renaming it New South Wales (he thought it resembled the south coast of Wales in Britain). Cook had in total led three expeditions into the Pacific, during which he reached Tahiti and every major South Pacific island group, sailed around New Zealand, accurately charting the coasts of its two main islands, and discovered and explored Hawaii (where he was killed in 1779).

Between 1788 and 1868 (when transportation ended), around 162,000 convicts were transported to penal settlements in New South Wales, Van Diemen's Land (Tasmania – settled in 1803) and Western Australia (founded in 1829). Some 137,000 of the convicts were men, mostly young poor men from industrial centres, many of them convicted thieves with just seven-year sentences or less; 25,000 were females.

Convicts at first formed the majority of the colony's population, although free settlers began arriving in 1793, and in 1800 outnumbered convicts in New South Wales. Conditions for convicts were harsh, although only about 15 per cent of them were sentenced to actual prisons or chain gangs. After 1801, good conduct could lead to 'tickets of leave' that entitled convicts to work for wages or even pardons, so long as they never returned to Britain. Transportation ended in 1868 when the population of Australia – at 1 million – could support itself without the need for any more convicts.

250 NATIONS OF ABORIGINAL PEOPLE

In 1788, the Aboriginal population of Australia existed as 250 individual nations, each with its own or multiple languages (200 of which are now extinct), the population estimated at anything between 300,000 and 750,000. Disease brought in by European settlers, in particular smallpox, had a devastating effect, killing as much as 40–60 per cent of the Aboriginal population in south-eastern Australia.

Many aboriginal people were murdered or treated brutally by white settlers (the extent of violence is still subject to debate), or forcibly removed from their lands. The Aboriginal population in Tasmania was almost entirely wiped out. The historian Phillip Knightley estimates that over a period of 150 years the Aboriginal population declined from an estimated 300,000 in 1788 to 75,000. In 2011, the estimated 670,000 indigenous Australians represented 3 per cent of Australia's population.

ARMIES OF 250,000

Napoleon Bonaparte

The French Revolutionary and Napoleonic Wars, fought between 1792 and 1815, saw France fighting various coalitions of European states, starting with Austria, Prussia, Spain, the United Provinces and Britain.

Although Admiral Horatio Nelson defeated a combined French and Spanish fleet at the Battle of Trafalgar in 1805, establishing Britain as the world's foremost naval power, Napoleon Bonaparte dominated mainland Europe. Fighting to defend and spread republicanism and then to extend his influence in Europe, Napoleon defeated a combined Austrian and Russian army at the battle of Austerlitz in December 1805.

The Revolutionary and Napoleonic wars typically involved large armies made possible by France's mass enlistment of its male citizens from 1798 – 1.3 million Frenchmen were conscripted between 1800 and 1812. After 1800, Napoleon routinely commanded armies of 250,000; fifty years before, armies that fought in Europe were generally no bigger than 60,000–70,000 troops.

Napoleon's 'Grande Armée' reached its maximum size of 600,000 men with the invasion of Russia in 1812. The French defeated the Russians at the Battle of Borodino in 1812, and took Moscow, but were then forced to retreat westwards, while 5,000–6,000 soldiers a day died from cold, starvation, disease and battles with Russians. It is estimated that 400,000 soldiers died in Russia, 220,000 from disease, many from typhus fever or dysentery. (Typhus epidemics are common occurrences during war: the first recorded instance was during the Plague of Athens in 430 BCE.)

Thereafter, the military strength of the French never fully recovered, and in 1814 Napoleon was forced to abdicate. He briefly retook power in 1815 but was defeated by Prussian, British and Belgian forces at the Battle of Waterloo.

NAPOLEON'S 100 DAYS

Napoleon's abdication in 1814 had led to exile on the tiny island of Elba off the west coast of Italy. After ten months, Napoleon escaped back to France, rallied support as he crossed the Alps, and arrived in Paris on 20 March 1815. For a brief period, known as the Hundred Days, he overthrew the restored King Louis XVIII, set up a political regime and mustered around 280,000 men, but suffered his final defeat at the Battle of Waterloo on 18 June 1815.

Again Napoleon was forced to abdicate, and this time the British authorities sent him to the remote island of St Helena, 1,950 km (1,200 miles) west of the south-western coast of Africa, where he died in 1821. The period of a hundred days, which usually refers to Napoleon's return to Paris on 20 March 1815 to the second restoration of King Louis XVIII on 8 July 1815, was in fact 111 days.

5 GREAT POWERS OF EUROPE

The defeat of Napoleon was followed by the Congress of Vienna, a peace conference held between 1814 and 1815. It established a new balance of power in Europe, centred on the five 'Great Powers': Britain, France, Prussia, Austria and Russia. The political map was redrawn, with France losing all its recent conquests and a new king, Louis XVIII, reinstated; republican Holland was reunited with Belgium under one king; and Poland and Italy redistributed among the Great Powers. The settlement is credited with preventing widespread European war for nearly a century.

4 CENTS AN ACRE

In 1803, the US government, under the newly inaugurated President Thomas Jefferson, struck one of the best bargains in history. Napoleon, now at war with Britain and keen to shed territory he could not defend, sold a vast region known as Louisiana for $15 million. At a stroke, 2,144,520 square km (828,000 square miles) of land – stretching from the Mississippi River to the Rockies and from the Gulf of Mexico to Canada – were added to US territory. This represented at least double the area gained from the British in 1783, and increased the size of the United States by 140 per cent, drawing settlement westwards. Ultimately, thirteen states would be carved out of the land, in part or as a whole, for a price that works out as roughly four cents an acre.

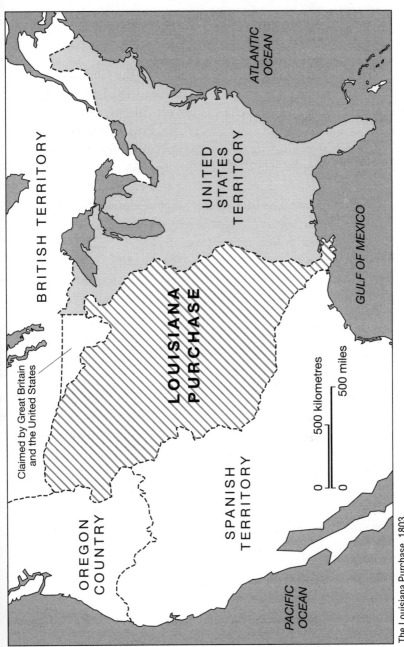

The Louisiana Purchase, 1803.

7,000 BRITISH VOLUNTEERS IN LATIN AMERICA

The revolutions of North America and France also inspired the Spanish colonies in South America to fight for independence. The trigger for conflict arose in 1808, after Napoleon deposed the Spanish monarchy in the Peninsular War, leading to political instability and war throughout the Spanish domains of America.

Among those who signed up to fight for the liberation of Spanish America were around 7,000 British and Irish volunteers, many of them veterans of the Napoleonic Wars in need of military employment (*The Times* in 1817 estimated there were half a million ex-soldiers out of a population of 25 million). Some of the volunteers, however, were likely motivated by the liberal vision of a free and united South America, as espoused by Simón Bolívar, the great Venezuelan general who led Venezuela, Colombia, Ecuador, Peru and Bolivia to independence from the Spanish Empire.

Under Bolívar, the British and Irish volunteers fought in the Battle of Boyacá on 7 August 1819, after which Colombia (then known as New Granada) was proclaimed independent. Six hundred British soldiers also played a crucial role at Carabobo on 24 June 1821, securing an against-the-odds victory against Spanish forces and subsequent independence for Venezuela. Over 100 of the British troops died during the battle, including their commander Thomas Ferrier. Bolívar described the British Legion as *Salvadores de mi Patria*, 'the saviours of my country'. Out of the 7,000 British and Irish volunteers, 3,000 died during battle or from disease, 500 remained in the country, while the rest returned to Britain.

Bolívar subsequently went south to help the independence movement in other colonies under the leadership of José de

San Martin, who with his second-in-command Bernardo O'Higgins had defeated the Spanish forces in Chile, leading to its independence in 1818. In 1822, Bolívar helped expel the remaining Spanish forces, becoming its dictator in 1824. In the following year, he founded a republic in Upper Peru, later named Bolivia in his honour. By 1830, Spain no longer had any control over the South American continent. Argentina declared independence in 1816, and Mexico in 1821. Brazil became independent of Portugal in 1822.

250,000 TONS OF PIG IRON

The process of industrialization that transformed Britain in the eighteenth and nineteenth centuries would soon spread to Europe and around the world. From around 1820 an intense industrial revolution took place in many parts of Western Europe, particularly in the coal-rich areas of Germany, northern France and Belgium.

Pig-iron production soared in Germany, from just 40,000 tons in 1825 to 250,000 tons by the early 1850s. Coal and iron manufacture doubled in France within the same time span. Unification in Germany in 1871 spurred the rapid spread of the steel, chemicals and electrical industries.

Railways also spread across Europe and the world. The US completed the first transcontinental railroad in 1869, having built 50,000 miles of rail track (compared with Britain's 6,000 miles of rail track built between 1820 and 1850). In fact, industrialization in the US grew exponentially, its economy also driven by the production of cotton and textiles (right up to the First World War the export of raw cotton from the South still made up 25 per cent of US exports). By 1900, the

US was the world's leading industrial power, producing 24 per cent of the world's manufacturing output (compared to Britain's 18 per cent).

MARX'S 6 STAGES OF HISTORY

Industrialization created great wealth for some, in particular industrialists, professionals and merchants, whereas life for many ordinary workers was still harsh. Over the course of the nineteenth century disparities between rich and poor grew in the industrial societies of Europe – in Prussia in 1854, a 21 per cent share of income went to the top 5 per cent of the population; by 1913 this had risen to 43 per cent. In Britain, between 1780 and 1830, when the population doubled, output per labourer grew by 25 per cent but wages rose by just 5 per cent.

Throughout Europe people demanded political and social reform. Two leading thinkers were the German philosophers Karl Marx (1818–83) and Friedrich Engels (1820–95), who set out their ideas in the *Communist Manifesto*, published in 1848. They believed that economic forces shaped all history, and identified six successive stages: the primitive communism of hunter-gatherer families; evolving into ancient autocratic monarchies with a slave-owning ruling class; then feudalism; capitalism; socialism; and finally pure communism (when there is no money or private property, no government, laws or distinctions of class).

Their belief that a socialist state, based on common ownership and production, could only be achieved through violent revolution alarmed many middle-class liberals of Europe, many of whom chose to work within their existing regimes, provided they had a voice in government.

Discontent and unemployment among the working class of Europe, alongside an upsurge in nationalism and demands from the middle classes for constitutional reform, led to a series of revolts in 1848, beginning in France and spreading to much of Europe, including Hungary, Austria, Ireland, Switzerland, Denmark, and many German and Italian states. Within a year counter-revolutionary forces had restored order. The revolutions had achieved little in terms of permanent political change, but their governments had been forced to listen to the voice of the people and the concept of absolute monarchy had been tacitly abandoned.

8 NEW NATION STATES IN EUROPE

Between 1830 and 1905, nationalism – the concept that groups of people united by race, language or history should rule their own country – became a potent force in Europe. Eight nations achieved independence or unity. Belgium secured independence from Holland in 1830; following the destruction of the Turkish–Egyptian fleet by an allied fleet of Great Powers in 1827, Greece broke away from the failing Ottoman Empire in 1832 and Romania followed in 1859; Italy became a unified state in 1861, Germany in 1871; Bulgaria and Serbia were recognized in 1878, and Norway in 1905.

2.5 PER CENT OF ITALIANS SPEAK ITALIAN

In much of Europe, however, there was little mass support for nationalism. Most populations maintained local or regional loyalties, and few moved far from the district they were born in. In Italy in 1861, only 2.5 per cent of Italians spoke Italian: French was spoken in the north, and various other dialects in the rest of the country. Italian was seen as a literary language.

So the Italian statesman Count Cavour recognized that unity in Italy could only be achieved with foreign intervention and via military force. An alliance with Napoleon III of France helped to expel the Austrians. By 1870, after Giuseppe Garibaldi had secured victory over a Bourbon king in Sicily and Southern Italy, all of Italy was united.

Prussia's chief minister, Otto von Bismarck (1815–98), similarly recognized that Germany, dominated by Prussia, could only be unified through war. The Austro-Prussian War of 1866 brought defeat for Austria and extended German territory. In 1870, Bismarck goaded Napoleon III into war, leading to defeat for France and its loss of Alsace and Lorraine to the Germans. On a tide of nationalist excitement, the German states in 1871 proclaimed their union under their new emperor Wilhelm I, with Bismarck their chancellor. The new empire of Germany soon became the dominant power in continental Europe.

HUNDREDS OF MILLIONS MIGRATE

The growth in colonial empires, industrialization and improved transportation (in particular ocean-going steam ships and the railway) led to a surge of migration in the nineteenth century. Emigrants sought employment, cheap land and better lives, or fled persecution (the mass emigration of Russian Jews saw more than 2 million leave Russia between 1880 and 1920, many bound for North America).

The nineteenth century saw the migration of 51 million Russians to Central Asia, Manchuria and Siberia (7 million

Russians to Siberia between 1801 and 1914); 52 million Indians and Chinese to South-East Asia, Australasia and the Indian Ocean rim; and 58 million Europeans to the Americas.

Of the migrant Europeans, the vast majority – around 36 million between 1800 and 1917 – went to North America, many of them British, Irish and German. Six million Europeans went to South America, in particular to Argentina and Brazil, where Spanish, Portuguese, Italians and Germans settled; and another 5 million – mainly British and French – went to Canada.

⅓ OF IRISH POPULATION DEPENDENT ON LUMPER POTATO

The last great subsistence crisis to affect Europe was the potato blight, which in the nineteenth century was first recorded in North America, spreading to all potato-growing countries in Europe. Between 1845 and 1851 it hit Ireland the hardest, as potatoes had become the mainstay of the Irish diet – one third of the population depended on the Irish Lumper potato. Destruction of the potato crops led to widespread famine and more than 1 million deaths, while another million emigrated.

Many emigrants went to England, Scotland, Canada and Australia, but most settled in North America, accelerating a trend that had started before the famine. By 1850, the Irish made up a quarter of the population of many US cities. In 2010, 34.7 million US residents claimed Irish ancestry, a number more than seven times the population of Ireland itself (4.58 million).

'54–40 OR FIGHT!'

The slogan 'Fifty-four forty or fight!' excited the US public during a dispute between British and US claims over the northwest Pacific area of North America. American expansionists claimed that the US had title to the entire Oregon Country up to latitude 54°40′ north. Eventually, the Oregon Treaty of 1846 struck a compromise boundary at the 49th parallel, and this largely remains as the western part of the US–Canada boundary.

Since the purchase of the Louisiana territories from the French in 1803 (see page 126), the United States had been establishing itself further into the American continent, its expansion west towards the Pacific Coast representing one of the biggest migrations in history. In 1820, Florida, Missouri and Maine were added to the Union; the Republic of Texas was annexed in 1845, and US victory in the Mexican-American war of 1846–48 gained California and New Mexico. By 1850, half of America's 23 million people lived beyond the Appalachians, a mountain range that in 1815 was effectively the border of the US, with only one in seven people living west of it.

The moral ideology of 'manifest destiny', first coined in 1845 by a newspaper editor to urge the annexation of Texas, provided another catchphrase for supporters of expansionism with the claim that it was America's duty to remake and settle in the West. In the later nineteenth century, millions of Americans and European immigrants settled in these newly acquired lands, and by the end of the Spanish-American War in 1898 the Union had purchased Alaska from the Russians (for $7.2 million – roughly 2 cents an acre), annexed Hawaii and taken control of a number of overseas territories, including Puerto Rico, Guam and the Philippines.

90,000 NATIVE AMERICANS

As migrants advanced west in North America, native Americans were uprooted and moved from their homelands, and many died as a result of war, disease or loss of livelihood. Between 1830 and 1895 the number of Native Americans fell from 2 million to 90,000, while around 70 million buffalo (a main source of livelihood for Plains Indians) were slaughtered.

Distorted depictions of the 'Wild West' convey the impression that marauding Indians constantly attacked westward migrants. In fact, of the half a million people who passed through Indian territories in wagon trains between 1840 and 1860, it is estimated that just 362 died from attacks from hostile natives. Settlers of America's West were in the main farmers, and not the movies' gun-slinging cowboys: farmers outnumbered cowboys by about 1,000 to 1.

21 MILES OF ELECTRIC CABLE

The Crimean War (1853–6) fought by Russia against the Allied forces of Turkey, Britain, France and Sardinia, saw the first use of the telegraphic cable in a war environment. By the end of the war, 21 miles of cable had been laid in the Crimea, connecting eight telegraph offices on a circuit, with 340 miles of submarine cable laid from Varna to Balaclava in April 1855.

News from correspondents reached all nations involved in the conflict, providing its citizens with up-to-date information as never before seen in times of war. By 1855, news of the Crimea could reach London within hours (only forty years earlier it had taken two days for Wellington's victory over Napoleon at Waterloo to reach London). The Crimean War was also the first to be extensively documented with written reports and photography.

The Allies eventually won, with Russia signing a peace treaty in 1856. The loss of life, however, was immense: 25,000 British, 100,000 French and up to 1 million Russians died, mostly of disease and neglect.

20,000 CHESTS OF OPIUM

On the banks of the Pearl River outside Humen Town in southern China, a Chinese commissioner named Lin Zexu oversaw the destruction of 20,000 chests of opium. It was such a vast amount (over 1,000 tons) that it took a team of 500 over three weeks to destroy the opium by throwing it into pits filled with lime, salt and sea water, then trampling on it, before letting the residue trickle into the South China Sea.

Under the orders of the Chinese emperor, Lin had been trying to eradicate the trade in foreign opium, most of it shipped by the British East India Company, resulting in around 10 million opium addicts in China by 1830. At the same time, the British were buying huge quantities of tea from China, around 10.4 million kg (23 million pounds) a year in 1800, creating a trade imbalance that the British attempted to offset by selling Indian opium to China – sales grew five-fold between 1821 and 1837.

The British resented Lin's seizure and sent a force of sixteen warships to besiege Canton (Guangzhou), capturing Shanghai in 1842. The Treaty of Nanjing (the first of what the Chinese call the 'unequal treaties') granted an indemnity to Britain and the cession of Hong Kong. When the Qing authorities later refused to negotiate more favourable terms for the Nanjing Treaty, the Second Opium War broke out between 1856 and1860, and this time French forces joined in. After Beijing was occupied, the Chinese agreed to the Treaty of Tianjin in 1860, and which opened another ten ports to Western trade.

20 MILLION LEFT DEAD

As the Second Opium War broke out, much of central China was being ravaged by the most destructive civil war in history. Between 1850 and 1864 over 20 million people lost their lives – more than double the losses among all combatant nations in the First World War.

The Taiping rebellion began under the leadership of the Christian convert Hong Xiuquan, who claimed to be the younger brother of Jesus Christ sent to reform China. Beginning in Guangzi province, the religious sect known as the God Worshippers attracted impoverished peasants and workers (many of them opium addicts). A band of a few thousand grew to more than 1 million fanatical and extremely disciplined soldiers, the uprising spreading to the central and lower Yangtze regions. The rebels captured the city of Nanjing in 1853 (renaming it 'Heavenly City'), and thereafter controlled a large part of southern China.

Western powers helped the Manchu government in their fight against the rebellion, with the Manchu granting them better port facilities for trade and legalized opium sales (see above). The capture of Nanjing in 1864 led to the crushing of the resistance, although the Qing dynasty never fully recovered from the civil war.

1 IN 15 US SERVICEMEN DIE

The most lethal war in US history, the American Civil War, cost a possible 620,000 lives (a recent estimate puts the figure as high as 750,000), more than the American death toll in the First and Second World Wars, which had a combined total of 534,000, and more than any US war before or since. During the American Civil War, soldiers had roughly a 1 in 15 chance of dying in battle (the risk was 1 in 50 in the War of Independence; 1 in 45 in the Mexican War; 1 in 89 in the First World War, and 1 in 56 in the Second World War) and a quarter of all white males of serving age in the Confederacy were killed.

The Civil War had been fought between two geographic sections of the US: the industrialized North, twenty-three northern and western states, which had for the most part abandoned slavery, and eleven agricultural slave-owning states of the South. The presidential election of Abraham Lincoln, a candidate from the anti-slavery Republican Party, in 1860 prompted the southern states to split from the Union and form the Confederate States of America, seeking to win recognition as an independent nation. The North fought to preserve the Union.

3,841,000 COTTON BALES

Primary among the Confederates' concerns was that a federal government would lead to the prohibition of slavery in the South. Just as the abolition of slavery was taking hold in the North (as early as 1804, seven northern states had abolished it), the more agricultural south saw a revival of the cotton industry as a result of new machinery (such as the cotton gin). Between 1810 and 1860 cotton production jumped from 178,000 bales to 3,841,000 bales, which simultaneously led to a marked increase in the use of black slaves in the South, rising from 1,190,000 to almost 4 million. The first six states to secede from the Union had the highest percentage of slaves in their populations – a total of 48.8 per cent.

INCOME TAX RAISES 21 PER CENT OF WAR REVENUE

Fighting began in 1861 when Confederate troops opened fire on Union forces at Fort Sumter in South Carolina. On 21 July, some 30,000 Union forces were driven back from Manassas in Virginia by Confederate forces led by General 'Stonewall' Jackson and General Beauregard. Despite initial victories by the Confederates, however, the South was gradually worn down, as its economy collapsed under the weight of heavy inflation.

The North had a much greater population – 22 million compared with the South's 9 million – and housed four-fifths of America's industry. In the first eighteen months of war, the North imposed the first income tax in US history, which ultimately raised 21 per cent of its war revenue, along with the first paper currency ('greenbacks').

The South had a less developed fiscal and banking system. It paid for the war by printing money, which led to soaring inflation – the price of salt in 1863, a staple for preserving food, rose as much as thirtyfold. The South was also more reliant on European imports, its economy severely impacted by the northern blockade of southern ports, which also cut its cotton exports by 90 per cent.

By 1863 Union forces had halted the Confederates' advance north at the Battle of Gettysburg. In April 1865, the supreme commander of the Union forces, General Ulysses S. Grant, began his final advance and on 9 April he received Confederate leader Robert E. Lee's surrender at Appomattox. Victory for the North ended the Confederacy, strengthened the federal government and led to the abolition of slavery in the US.

13TH AMENDMENT

The abolition of slavery was passed by the US Congress in March 1865, as outlined in the US constitution's thirteenth amendment: 'Neither slavery nor involuntary servitude, except as a punishment for crime whereof the party shall have been duly convicted, shall exist within the United States, or any place subject to their jurisdiction.'

133 SLAVES THROWN OVERBOARD

In 1840, the British artist J. M. W. Turner exhibited *The Slave Ship*, a painting that depicts a ship sailing through stormy waters with dead and dying human bodies in the water. He was inspired to paint it after reading about an event in 1781 in which the captain of the slave ship *Zong* had 133 slaves thrown overboard so that insurance payments could be collected. The painting's exhibition coincided with an anti-slavery conference, to be attended by Prince Albert and those committed to the abolition of slavery around the world.

Since the late eighteenth century, awareness over the brutal realities of slavery had grown, with religious groups in Britain campaigning for its abolition. By 1804, most northern states in the US had rejected the slave trade, and Britain (a major slave-trading nation) outlawed its practice by British merchants three years later. By 1833, the British had abolished it throughout the British Empire, the French in their colonies by 1848. Elsewhere, the trade went on, particularly in North America, Brazil and Cuba, where demand for cotton and sugar was high.

The American Civil War led to the abolition of slavery throughout the US in 1865, though Cuba and Brazil retained it throughout the 1870s – in fact, in 1870 there were still 1.5 million slaves in Brazil, many more than there had been in 1800. Cuba and Brazil finally abolished slavery in 1886 and 1888, and while this spelled the end of the Atlantic slave trade, Arab and African merchants still transported slaves to North and East Africa, a practice that continued until the twentieth century. A type of slavery in the form of forced labour still exists today, with human rights campaigners estimating that that there are still between 21 million and 30 million slaves across the world.

502 PAGES OF DARWIN'S *ON THE ORIGIN OF SPECIES*

On 24 November 1859, the first edition of Charles Darwin's *On the Origin of Species* was published. Containing fourteen chapters and 502 pages, the book provided a scientific explanation for his theory of evolution by natural selection. The first edition had a print run of 1,250 copies, and was followed by a second in 1860 with a print run of 3,000 – during Darwin's lifetime the book went through six extensively revised editions. (Only the fifth edition, published in 1869, contained the phrase 'survival of the fittest', as coined by the philosopher Herbert Spencer.)

Darwin had formulated his theory some twenty years earlier after a round-the-world voyage on HMS *Beagle* during 1837–9. The book caused a tremendous stir both within the scientific community and the public at large, shocking religious leaders and Victorian society with its assertion that humans and animals shared a common ancestry. Yet Darwin's work was to deeply influence Western society and thought, and remains central to the foundations of modern biology and evolutionary theory today.

40,000 American Millionaires

The industrialization of North America moved astonishingly fast between 1850 and 1900. Production, exports, railroad building and wealth grew exponentially as steel production rose from 13,000 tons a year to 11.3 million tons. By 1913, the US was producing a third of the world's manufactured goods, its total iron and steel production of 32 million tons only a little less than that of France, Britain, Germany and Russia combined.

Vast wealth ensued: the number of millionaires in the US rose from fewer than twenty in 1850 to 40,000 by the end of the century. Conversely, the disparity between rich and poor intensified, and the top 10 per cent of American households owned about four-fifths of the nation's wealth between 1860 and 1900. One of the richest families to emerge during the US's 'Gilded Age' were the Vanderbilts, who amassed a huge fortune from the shipping and railroad industries. The founder of the dynasty, Cornelius Vanderbilt, bequeathed a fortune of 100 million dollars on his death in 1877, and at one point controlled about 10 per cent of all the money in circulation in the US.

HEINZ 57

Advertisement for Heinz, 1910

In the late nineteenth century, the new innovation of canned food was soon associated with the German-American Henry John Heinz, who began selling horseradish, pickles and mustard, branching out into tomato ketchup in 1876.

In 1896, Heinz began using the '57 varieties' slogan, an idea that apparently came to him when he noticed a shoe advert in Manhattan with the heading '21 styles'. The number '57' simply appealed to him: 'There are so many illustrations of the psychological influence of that figure and its alluring significance to people of all ages and races that "58 Varieties" or "59 Varieties" did not appeal at all to me as equally strong.' Today Heinz claim to sell 650 million bottles of ketchup per year, which works out as two single-serve sachets of ketchup for every man, woman and child on the planet.

66 SKYSCRAPERS

The population of New York in the US rose from less than 1 million in 1860 to 4.8 million inhabitants in 1910. In 1902, some sixty-six skyscrapers were under construction in Lower Manhattan.

280 DAIMYO LANDHOLDINGS ABOLISHED

In 1854, Japan had been compelled to open up two of its ports to US trade, thereby ending a self-imposed isolation that since 1639 had stifled foreign contacts. Further treaties with other countries, among them Britain and Russia, led to open rebellion by a group of anti-Tokugawa samurai who overthrew the shogunate. The young Meiji Emperor Mutsuhito resumed formal imperial rule in January 1868, and a year later moved his capital from Kyoto to Edo (renaming it Tokyo).

Thereafter, in a bid to strengthen Japan so that it could resist Western domination, he began a series of modernizing reforms that profoundly and swiftly affected all aspects of Japanese social, political and economic life. His dismantling of the feudal daimyo (landholder) and samurai (warrior) system abolished more than 280 daimyo landholdings and replaced them with seventy-two Western-style districts, while the samurai lost many of their feudal privileges.

A centralized government based in Tokyo introduced conscription in 1872, marking the end of the samurai monopoly of military power. In the same year, compulsory elementary education was introduced, so that Japan became the most literate society in Asia, achieving almost 100 per cent literacy by 1900. In 1885, a cabinet government with a prime minister at its head was established (although still only 1 per cent of Japan's population could vote), and Japan's legal system and army were remodelled on Western lines.

By the end of the nineteenth century, Japan had become an equal of the European powers, able to defeat China in the Sino-Japanese War of 1894–5, forming an alliance with Britain in 1902, and further shocking Europe when she destroyed Russian troops on land and sea in the Russo-Japanese War of 1904–5.

PATENT NO. 174,465

Alexander Graham Bell at the unveiling of a plaque commemorating the 1876 invention of the telephone, Boston, US, 1916

In 1876, Alexander Graham Bell, a Scotsman living in the US, invented the telephone by using telegraph technology to transmit the sound of voices. The patent for his invention, no. 174,465, became the most valuable patent ever granted. Telephones were first installed in Boston City in 1877, and by the early 1880s there were 60,000 telephones in use across the US, rising to 285,000 in 1894, and sky-rocketing to 3,317,000 by 1904. By this time, Bell's telephone company, renamed American Telephone & Telegraph, was the largest company in America. When it was broken up in the 1980s, it was worth $149.5 billion, said to be more than General Motors, IBM, Ford, Xerox, General Electric and Coca-Cola combined.

1 PER CENT INSPIRATION AND 99 PER CENT PERSPIRATION

Thomas Edison (1847–1931) patented 1,093 inventions during his lifetime – proving his own maxim that genius is '1 per cent inspiration and 99 per cent perspiration'. His inventions included the motion picture camera, phonograph and long-lasting light bulb, although his success also lay in establishing systems that would lead to major new industry, much of which would revolutionize modern life.

His company, the Electrical Illuminating Company, established the first power plant in New York City, which in 1882 provided electricity to fifty-nine customers in lower Manhattan. By 1887, there were 121 Edison power stations in the US, and by 1900 electrical lighting had become the norm in most North American cities.

7 European Nations Carve Up Africa

Between 1881 and 1914, seven European nations – the French, British, Germans, Portuguese, Spanish, Belgians and Italians – occupied, annexed and colonized almost all of the African continent so that by the eve of the First World War, only Ethiopia (formerly Abyssinia) and Liberia remained independent.

Early exploration of Africa's interior had heightened the interest of European powers whose burgeoning industry was crying out for Africa's untapped resources of minerals, precious metals and cheap raw material. This, combined with intense rivalry and political tension between European nations, evident during the Berlin Conference of 1884–5, triggered a frenzied scramble for Africa. In 1870, European powers controlled just 10 per cent of Africa (Algeria ruled by France; the Cape Colony and Natal by Britain; and Angola by Portugal); by 1914, 90 per cent of the African continent was under European control.

Wars raged across west, central and eastern Africa as European nations, principally Britain, France and Germany, conducted military campaigns among themselves and against African nations. Despite fierce resistance from African nations and rulers, among them the Ashanti and Zulus, European forces, with their far superior firepower, gained the upper hand. By 1900, European states had added almost 10 million square miles of territory to their colonial possessions (the British alone controlled over 4 million square miles of land and 30 per cent of Africa's population). European possessions in Africa covered one-fifth of the land-mass of the globe.

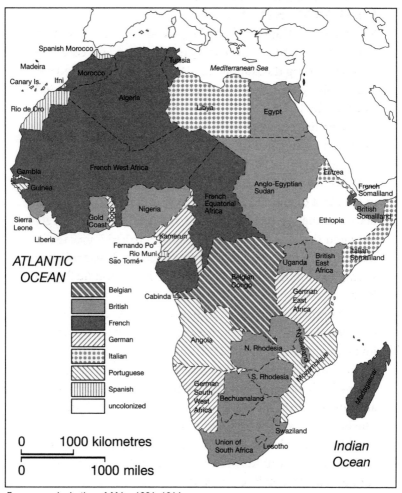

European colonization of Africa, 1881–1914

26,000 Boer Women and Children Killed

South Africa's Cape of Good Hope had been colonized by Dutch Boers ('boer' means farmer) since the seventeenth century. During the Napoleonic Wars, Britain colonized the Cape Colony, leading to the migration northwards of 12,000 Boers in the Great Trek between 1835 and 1843, in a bid to escape British control and its abolition of slavery. Soon after, the Boers established the two independent republics of the Transvaal and the Orange Free State.

When it was discovered that the Transvaal region was rich in gold and diamonds, British fortune hunters attempted to take over the region. This led to a bitter three-year struggle between the Boers and British between 1899 and 1902. Early Boer victories turned to defeat against a British military strength in South Africa of 500,000 men facing around 88,000 Boers.

Britain had waged a 'scorched earth' policy, under its commander-in-chief Horatio Herbert Kitchener, which involved destroying Boer farms and interning the civilian population (mainly women and children) in concentration camps. In these, more than 26,000 Boer women and children are estimated to have died, along with 13,000–20,000 Africans. The Boer War was the largest and costliest war that the British fought between the Napoleonic Wars and the First World War, with the loss of around 100,000 lives (20,000 of them British soldiers and 14,000 Boer troops).

WHITES GIVEN 90 PER CENT OF SOUTH AFRICA

South Africa was established as a self-governing dominion of the British Crown in 1910, a union made up of the former colonies of the Cape and Natal territories and former Dutch republics of Transvaal and Orange Free State.

New laws systematized anti-black legislation in much of the social and economic life of South Africa, as The Natives' Land Act of 1913 severely restricted the ownership of land by black people to 10 per cent, later marginally increased to 13 per cent. (Until the end of apartheid in 1991–2, approximately nine-tenths of the land in South Africa belonged exclusively to the white population.)

Only white males could vote in Transvaal and the Orange Free State, while the great majority of black people in the Cape and Natal were disenfranchised. In 1910, in the Cape, 85 per cent of voters were white, 10 per cent mixed race, and 5 per cent black. In response, middle-class black Africans founded the South African Native National Congress in 1912 (renamed the African National Congress in 1923), its specific goal the maintenance of voting rights for coloured and black Africans in the Cape.

From the 1940s, the ANC spearheaded the fight to eliminate apartheid in South Africa. It gained final political ascendancy in 1994 with the election of its president Nelson Mandela as the head of the South African government.

Nelson Mandela, 1918–2013

450 Million Taels of Fine Silver

In 1901, China signed a peace protocol with an alliance of nations who had sent military troops to China to end an uprising known as the Boxer Rebellion. Heavy fines were levied against China, which was required to pay 450 million taels (ounces) of fine silver (equating to US$330 million and £67 million at the exchange rate at the time) over thirty-nine years to the nations involved (France, Russia, Germany, Great Britain, Austria-Hungary, the United States, Japan and Italy).

This figure represented approximately two years of government revenue for China, and double the amount when interest payments were factored in. Taxes were subsequently increased, while existing commercial treaties were amended in favour of Western powers, with foreign troops stationed in Beijing and elsewhere.

The Boxer Rebellion had broken out in 1898 as a response to increasing foreign intervention in China (the uprising named after the discontents' 'Society of Righteous and Harmonious Fists'). Rebels had attacked foreign embassies, killing Europeans and Chinese Christians, until an allied force of 19,000 foreign soldiers arrived in August 1900. By the following month, the Empress Dowager Cixi had been forced to accept the harsh terms of the protocol.

End of 2,000 Years of Imperial Rule

The humiliating terms of the Boxer Protocol and the failure of the rebellion to eject the West led to a further weakening of the Qing dynasty and increasing support for revolution. In 1911, revolutionaries overthrew the Manchu dynasty, and their leader Sun Yat-sen was elected provisional president of the new Chinese republic. The forced abdication of the last Qing emperor Puri, aged six, ended 2,000 years of imperial rule in China.

½ THE POPULATION DENIED THE VOTE

Throughout the nineteenth century, women, who were largely denied voting rights, campaigned for universal suffrage. In Britain, women over thirty finally won the right to vote in 1918, a result of the campaigning work of the National Union of Women's Suffrage Societies, the more militant 'Suffragettes', as well as changing attitudes about the role of women brought about by the First World War (when 1.6 million women were in work, half of them in engineering).

Across the world, New Zealand had extended suffrage to women in 1893, followed by south Australia in 1895 (and 1902 in the federated Australia – although indigenous women and men were banned from voting until 1962). In the US state of Wyoming, women over twenty-one were given the vote in 1869, although it wasn't until the 1920s that women across the US attained voting rights. In Brazil, all restrictions to women's suffrage were removed in 1932.

Elsewhere, voting rights were given to women in Japan in 1945, Argentina 1947, India 1947, South Korea 1948, Chile 1949, Egypt 1956, Nigeria 1958, Uganda 1962, Kenya 1963, and in South Africa white women were granted the vote in 1930, women of all races in 1994. In the Middle East, certain countries lagged behind: Iran granted universal suffrage in 1963, Iraq in 1980, and women could still not vote in Saudi Arabia in 2014. In Europe, Finland was the first country to grant women suffrage in 1906, followed by Norway in 1913 and Russia (as a result of the Revolution) in 1917. Germany, Austria and Poland gained the vote for women just after the First World War, whereas France did not grant female suffrage until 1944, Belgium in 1948, and Switzerland was the last European country to grant equal voting for women in 1971.

'We Want 8, and We Won't Wait!'

On 10 February 1906, the world's media assembled in Portsmouth, England to watch the launch of the Royal Navy's new battleship, HMS *Dreadnought*. Hailed as 'the most deadly fighting machine ever launched in the history of the world', the ship displayed fearsome technology with ten 305-mm (12-inch) guns and steam turbine engines that enabled her to reach speeds of 21 knots (39 km/24 mph).

All other battleships were, at a stroke, deemed obsolete. The unveiling sparked a naval arms race around the world, as navies, particularly the German Imperial Navy, rushed to build Dreadnoughts and modernize their armed forces.

In Britain, the public clamoured for more Dreadnoughts, believing that only they could provide national security and prosperity. Naval propagandists cried: 'We want eight, and we won't wait!'

The resulting arms race was fuelled by growing tension between the Great Powers of Europe. A newly unified Germany, which had grown in industrial and military might in the late nineteenth century, had formed a triple alliance with Italy and Austria in 1882. France countered this by forming a dual alliance with Russia in 1884, and Great Britain concluded an 'Entente Cordiale' with France in 1904 and with Russia in 1907. This network of treaties and guarantees, intended to create stability in Europe, would ultimately drag all the Great Powers into world war.

10 TRAGIC DAYS

A series of revolts in Mexico City, held between 9 and 19 February 1913, are known in Mexican history as the Ten Tragic Days. With the city converted into a battle zone, civilian casualties were high. The fighting led to the execution of Mexican President Francisco Madero and his vice-president, while General Victoriana Huerta stepped up as president. The events formed part of the Mexican revolution, which had been instigated by Francisco Madero in 1910, following the fifth re-election of the Mexican dictator Porfirio Diaz, who had ruled since 1877.

Over time the revolution evolved from a struggle against the established order into a multi-sided civil war that spread across the whole of Mexico, killing some 2 to 3 million (out of a 1910 population of around 14 million). Its lasting legacy was the establishment of the National Revolutionary Party in 1929, which was led by politicians who supported social reform and, under a succession of names and leaders, held power until 2000.

8.5 MILLION MILITARY DEATHS

The assassination of the heir to the Austrian throne, Archduke Franz Ferdinand, by a teenage Bosnian Serb in the Serbian capital of Sarajevo on 28 June 1914, would spark the first ever world war. In a few weeks, all of the great European powers would be dragged into the conflict, with Russia, Japan, the United States, the Middle East and other regions also involved.

The Great War pitted the Allies, mainly France, Great Britain, Italy, Russia, Japan and the United States (from 1917), against the Central Powers, notably Germany, Austria-Hungary and Turkey.

The use of mechanized weaponry – from artillery and trench mortars to machine guns and hand grenades – led to unprecedented levels of casualties that dwarfed those of previous wars. Some 8.5 million soldiers died as a result of battlefield wounds or disease, artillery causing the most deaths, followed by small arms, then poison gas. The bayonet caused relatively few casualties. Numbers for civilian deaths – as war and the displacement of people led to disease, exposure, starvation and massacres – were even higher, at around 13 million.

400 MILES OF TRENCHES

When war broke out, German troops invaded and quickly overran most of Belgium, before sweeping into north-west France. Their advance was thrown back at the Battle of the Marne on 5 September 1914, when Allied troops forced them back to the River Aisne. The Germans never fully recovered their initiative, and thereafter both sides dug 650 km (400 miles) of defensive trenches from the Swiss border to the Belgian coast. This region of fighting became known as the Western Front.

Both sides then settled into three years of trench warfare, when machine guns and artillery made effective attacks from either side almost impossible, and likely to inflict an enormously high casualty rate. Two of the worst battles occurred in 1916: the French and Germans fought a long battle near Verdun, in which the Germans meant to 'bleed France white'. Over 714,000 troops were killed or wounded on both sides. At the same time, further north on the Somme, another struggle led to one of the bloodiest battles ever recorded, with well over 1 million soldiers killed, wounded or captured – approximately 650,000 Germans, 195,000 French and 420,000 British. On the first day's attack alone the British suffered 60,000 casualties and 20,000 deaths.

Despite the terrible loss of life, trench warfare on the Western Front resulted in little tactical or strategic advantage for either side: the line moved no more than 16 km (10 miles) either side.

¾ OF DEATHS CAUSED BY HEAD WOUNDS

For the first two years of the war, Allied soldiers were sent into battle with nothing more than a cloth cap on their heads. German troops were marginally better protected with the *pickelhaube*, a spiked leather helmet, but both offered scant protection against artillery fire and shrapnel. The resulting slaughter – around three out of four deaths caused by head wounds – prompted the British War Office to issue tin hats to all its troops in the spring of 1916. The US government followed when it joined the war in 1917, purchasing some 400,000 helmets (known as Doughboy helmets) for its servicemen.

92,000 Russian Soldiers Captured

During the first few days of the war in Eastern Europe, on 26–30 August 1914, the Russian 1st and 2nd Army fought against the German 8th Army at the Battle of Tannenberg. The Germans practically annihilated the Russian 2nd Army, with 92,000 Russians captured, 78,000 killed or wounded and only 10,000 escaping. In contrast, the Germans had just 13,000 casualties out of an army of 150,000.

The Germans also captured 350 Russian guns, which required sixty trains to transport back to Germany. The commander of the Russian 2nd Army, Alexander Samsonov, subsequently shot himself on 30 August. The Russians had better luck holding the Austrian province of Galicia before they were pushed back by Austro-Hungarian and German armies, losing Poland to the Germans in August 1915. By 1918 post-Revolutionary Russia had withdrawn from the conflict following the Treaty of Brest-Litovsk with Germany.

4 Million Colonial Troops

Fighting during the First World War also took place in the Middle East and Africa, with brief excursions in the Far East and Central Asia. Colonial troops were mobilized into armies across the theatres of war, with over 4 million non-white men fighting, 1.5 million of them from India and another 1.3 million from the British dominions of Canada, South Africa, New Zealand and Australia.

Between April 1915 and January 1916, Indian, Australian and New Zealand troops fought alongside the British and the French in an attempt to force the Ottoman Turks out of the war through the Gallipoli campaign, a landing in Turkey at the northern entrance to the Dardanelles. More than half of the 3,000 Indian troops were killed, 2,721 New Zealanders died (a quarter of those who landed), 8,709 Australians, 9,798 French, 34,072 British troops and 56,643 Ottoman Turks.

Both the British and French drew heavily upon their African colonies for manpower, and fielded some 500,000 African troops. Of the 1,186,000 French troops killed during the war, 71,000 of them came from the French colonies of Tunisia, Morocco, Algeria, Senegal and Madagascar (1 in 5 of West Africans from the French Empire died in the war, compared with 1 in 17 Frenchmen). Germany's African colonies, Togoland and Cameroon, were taken by Britain and France in 1914 and 1916, and South Africa conquered South-West Africa in 1915, though a German guerrilla campaign prevented the same success in East Africa.

3,870 FRENCH TANKS

Tanks were deployed on the battlefield for the first time during the First World War, initially by the British, who used the first tank in battle on 16 September 1916 during the Somme offensive. By the end of the war, the British had produced some 2,636 tanks, the French even more – 3,870. The Germans were never convinced of its merits, and fielded just twenty.

$1 MILLION A MINUTE

In the spring of 1918, the Germans launched a massive campaign on the Western Front, assembling 3.5 million soldiers (many transferred from the Eastern Front, after fighting in Russia had ceased in February 1918). However, backed by reinforcements from America – 200,000 arrived in 1917, rising to 1.8 million in 1918 – the Allies held their line and counter-attacked, finally piercing the 'Hindenburg Line' in September 1918.

The arrival of a seemingly inexhaustible supply of fresh and well-fed Americans seriously dented German morale. During the first three hours of the American offensive at the end of September 1918, more artillery was fired than during the whole of the US Civil War – about a million dollars' worth a minute.

This massive autumn offensive, combined with Britain's naval blockade of Germany, which seriously depleted Germany's stock of raw materials and foodstuffs, brought a quick end to hostilities. The armistice came into effect on 11 November 1918.

200,000 Petrograd Workers Strike

In Russia, the First World War had resulted in a heavy loss of life (around 1.7 million men). To finance the war, the government had simply printed money, which led to sky-high inflation and food shortages in many of its cities.

In two years, prices of essential items rose in Moscow by 131 per cent, and in Petrograd (now St Petersburg) by 150 per cent, and by 1917 prices were four times their level in 1914. During the severe winter of 1916–17, angered by the soaring prices and the daily, desperate search for food and fuel, thousands of women in Petrograd took to the streets demanding bread. The next day, on 24 February, between 100,000 and 200,000 workers went on strike, many of them calling for the overthrow of the Tsar. By 25 February, the city was paralysed, and when the army defied orders to suppress the uprising, Tsar Nicolas II was forced to abdicate on 2 March, ending over 300 years of Romanov rule.

Thereafter, a committee of the Duma (Parliament) appointed a liberal Provisional Government, which soon found itself opposed by Vladimir Lenin's Bolshevik Party. In October 1917, Lenin organized a coup, seizing the Winter Palace in Petrograd, and the Bolshevik Party seized power. It promised the Russian people 'peace, bread and land'. The first was secured by the Germans via the Treaty of Brest-Litovsk in March 1918, a brutal but short-lived treaty that forced Russia to cede 60 million people, including the Baltic States, to Germany.

Civil war ensued between the Red Army (the Bolsheviks) and the White Army (the more conservative anti-Bolshevik Russians). Lenin used state terror in the form of torture and execution to suppress opposition and started to transform Russia in line with Marxist principles, putting all land and industry under state control. The Russian Communist Party, as the Bolsheviks called themselves from 1918, gained supremacy and established the Soviet Union in 1922.

INFLUENZA TYPE A (H1N1)

Just as the world was recovering from the devastations of the First World War, one of the worst pandemics in history broke out. The new influenza virus, named influenza type A subtype H1N1, is now known to have caused 25 million deaths across the world (some estimates put the toll at 40–50 million).

Though popularly known as Spanish flu, the virus originated in Kansas, US, in early March 1918. It spread around the world the following winter, following a mutation. Once contracted it proliferated fast, killing up to 20 per cent of those infected, often just two days after symptoms appeared. In India, 12.5 million people lost their lives, in Indonesia 1.5 million (out of a population of 30 million), in the US approximately 675,000, and over 200,000 in Britain. The virus killed approximately 3 per cent of the world's population.

5-Year Plans

After Vladimir Lenin's death in 1924, Joseph Vissarionovich Dzhugashvili, who called himself Stalin ('man of steel'), took control of the Russian Communist Party. In a drive to industrialize and modernize the Soviet Union, he launched a series of five-year plans, ordering the collectivization of farms and the rapid development of industry.

The first Five-Year Plan (five years would allow for fluctuations in the harvest) came in 1928–32, the second in 1933–7, the third in 1938–42. The plans focussed on heavy industry: iron and steel, machine tools, armaments, and huge hydroelectric plants. In terms of industrial output, it worked – electricity generation rose tenfold between 1928 and 1941, steel and coal quadrupled, and the average annual growth rate during these years was 10 per cent. The Soviet Union had become a major industrial nation, one that could stand up to invasion during the Second World War.

But Soviet citizens paid a high price. For every ton of steel produced between 1929 and 1932, nineteen people died. Millions who resisted giving up land and livestock were shot or sent to Gulag labour camps. The government's seizure of grain in the early 1930s led to famine and the loss of many more millions – in

Soviet Ukraine 10 million peasants starved to death in 1932–3.

Further political repression between 1935 and 1938 led to large-scale purges of peasants, government officials, Red Army leaders (80 per cent of all colonels, 55 per cent of divisional and brigade commanders, 43 per cent of all other officer ranks) and members of the Communist Party. Over 10 million people were sent to labour camps or executed during Stalin's Great Purge.

1 IN 5 OWN AN AUTOMOBILE

During the 1920s, America enjoyed a period of economic prosperity, with unemployment dropping below 2 per cent and its economy growing at a rate of around 7 per cent a year. Wartime loans to Britain and France had made the US a major overseas investor (half of it in Europe), and turned New York into a major world money market. The subsequent fall in national debt enabled taxes to be cut again and again, and the United States became the world's leading exporter, with nearly one-sixth of global exports in 1929.

Economic prosperity also saw increasing consumer demand for household goods, such as radio, fridges and most notably cars, and a doubling of electrical consumption. Automobile production, spearheaded by Henry Ford (see next page), more than doubled during the decade, so that by 1930, 1 in 5 Americans owned a car (equating to one car per household) – a figure that Britain would not reach until the 1960s. Today the average is 2.8 for every US household.

90 Minutes to Make a Car

Model T Ford on display, 1908

By 1920, Henry Ford had revolutionized the US car industry, having first produced his Model T in 1908. By 1914, the car cost less than $500 to buy and soaring demand for it had led to a production of half a million a year. Assembly-line production enabled Ford to produce his cars in large numbers, reducing the time required to make each car at Ford's Detroit plant from twelve and a half hours to just over ninety minutes.

International Trade Slumps by 60 Per Cent

The optimism of the 1920s came to an abrupt end with the Wall Street Crash of 1929. An overheated market caused by the easy-credit policies of the US federal banks (by 1929 average household debt in the US had risen from 5 per cent in 1900 to nearly 10 per cent in 1929) had led to over-speculation by investors. Shares tumbled as panic selling took hold – 16 million shares changed hands on Black Tuesday, 29 October (a figure not surpassed for another forty years).

The ensuing Great Depression, as the US economy plunged into deep recession, shut down factories, bankrupted farmers, and closed 1 in 5 banks. Hundreds of thousands lost their homes and around 14 million their jobs. US banks were forced to call in their European loans and raise tariffs, and countries around the world were hit hard as international trade slumped by 60 per cent. Unemployment rates hit 25 per cent in Britain, 40 per cent in Germany, and with a 40 per cent decline in industrial production worldwide, the falling demand for raw materials severely affected countries in South America, the Far East and Africa.

Some economies began to recover in the mid-1930s, although for many, including the US, the effects of the Depression lasted until the end of the Second World War. Nothing could compare with the severity of the Great Depression until the financial crisis of 2007–8, when debt levels in the US again rose. (Usually standing at 150 per cent of GDP, debt levels rose just before the Depression to 200 per cent; in 2011 they were 400 per cent.)

GANDHI'S 24-DAY SALT MARCH

On 12 March 1930, the Hindu spiritual leader Mahatma Gandhi and seventy-nine supporters embarked upon a 380-km (240-mile) walk from Ahmedabad in Gujarat, India, arriving at Dandi on the Arabian Sea twenty-five days later. Once there, and under the eyes of the world's press, Gandhi picked up salty mud on the seashore and boiled it to make salt. After that, he continued southward along the coast, drawing in supporters and addressing meetings until he was arrested on 5 May 1930.

Gandhi's protest was meant to embarrass the British authorities whose taxing of salt, while providing just 8.2 per cent of the British Raj tax revenue, tended to hurt the poorest Indians most. The event drew worldwide attention to India's growing independence movement, spurred on after the Amritsar Massacre in 1919 when British Gurkha forces fired on a large crowd of non-violent protesters, killing 372 and wounding over 1,200 people.

Thereon the Indian National Congress, led by Gandhi, gained mass support, the Salt March leading to large-scale acts of civil disobedience by hundreds of thousands across India. The government kept control, but the Congress continued its call for outright independence.

By the time of independence in 1947, fatal clashes between Hindus and Muslims compelled the partitioning of the subcontinent into the self-ruling dominions of India and Pakistan. Around 15 million

Mahatma Gandhi en route to breaking the Salt Laws, 1930

Hindus, Muslims and Sikhs were forced to move either side of the demarcated border, the biggest such forced removal of people in history. The newly formed governments were unequipped to deal with such huge numbers of migrants. Violence broke out, and as many as 1 million people were slaughtered in communal massacres.

80,000 ON MAO'S LONG MARCH

In 1934–5, an army of 80,000 fought its way north on a year-long journey, famously known as the Long March, from the Chinese province of Jiangxi to Shaanxi province. The army was led by the Marxist revolutionary leader Mao Zedong, who with Zhu De in 1931 had set up a Chinese Communist republic in the Jiangxi province of southern China. Having resisted several attempts by the Kuomintang (Nationalist Party), led by Chiang Kai-shek, to remove them, they were finally forced to retreat in 1934.

Taking a circuitous route north (to avoid Kuomintang territory) over very difficult terrain, the distance covered is estimated at between 4,528 km and 12,875 km (3,000 and 8,000 miles); Mao declared it was the larger of the two figures. Only 20,000 completed the journey (most of them lost through desertion, starvation and disease, although there were also battles along the route). The Long March came to seal the prestige of Mao, who set up communist headquarters in Yan'an and continued to resist the Kuomintang.

During the second Sino-Japanese War (1937–45) the Communists fought hard against the Japanese and continued to expand their influence, so that by the end of the war around 96 million people in China were under Communist control. Civil war against the Kuomintang ended in victory for the Chinese Communist Party, which proclaimed the People's Democratic Republic of China in 1949, under Mao as its first head of state. The Long March has been a constant theme of communist propaganda ever since, though some claim that Mao's role in the march has been exaggerated.

2 MILLION NAZI PARTY MEMBERS

A Nazi rally, during the 1936 Olympic Games at the Lustgarten, Berlin, Germany

Staggering inflation in Germany – a US dollar worth 50 marks in 1922 was worth 2.5 trillion marks by 1924 – combined with recession and high unemployment in the post-Wall Street Crash era had resulted in economic deprivation and social turmoil in Germany. It was against this backdrop that the National Socialist German Workers' Party, or Nazi Party, rose to power.

Becoming leader in July 1921, the Austrian-born ex-First World War corporal Adolf Hitler drew support by promising to create jobs, restore national pride, and repudiate the humiliating terms of the peace treaty after the First World War, the Treaty of Versailles. His blaming of the economic crisis on Bolsheviks and Jewish financiers also resonated with a wide electorate.

By the time the party took power in 1933, the Nazi Party membership had grown to 2 million – Hitler's powerful oratory at mass rallies swaying people to the Nazi cause. As Chancellor, Hitler swiftly established a one-party dictatorship, eliminating his rivals and appointing himself Führer (leader) of the German Reich (state) in 1934. Thereafter, Hitler rebuilt the economy by pouring money into the army and public works, introduced a ruthless secret police and took total control of the country.

1 Per Cent of the Population Jewish

Central to Nazi ideology was the belief in the superiority of the German race, whose domination could only be achieved by the purging of 'weaker groups', which included Jews, Communists, Gypsies, homosexuals and the mentally disabled. Hitler targeted Jews in particular, and on coming to power immediately excluded them from German society. The Nuremberg Laws of 1935 deprived Jews of citizenship, Jewish businesses were confiscated, and in 1938, in an event known as Kristallnacht, Jewish synagogues and shops were attacked and looted.

Jewish people numbered 200,000, just 1 per cent of the German population, but the prominence of wealthy Jewish families in commerce, banking and industry caused resentment among other Germans – 5 out of the 29 wealthiest German financiers and bankers were Jewish. The German occupation of Poland (see page 157) immediately swelled the number of Jewish people under German control to 2 million, rising to a total of 5 million in 1941 when Germany took control of the Baltic States and the western Soviet Union.

40,000 JOIN THE INTERNATIONAL BRIGADE

A military coup in 1936 staged by a group of conservative generals against the socialist Republican government of Spain led to a violent conflict known as the Spanish Civil War. Between 17 July 1936 and 28 March 1939, approximately 1 million people lost their lives (600,000 on the battlefield).

The soldier General Francisco Franco commanded the rebel forces, known as the Nationalists, and won the support of Italy's fascist regime and the German Nazis. The Republican government was aided by the Soviet Union as well as by thousands of liberal-minded men and women from other countries. This International Brigade of volunteers was made up of 40,000 foreigners, among them 10,000 Frenchmen, 5,000 Germans, 4,000 Poles, 3,500 Italians, and 2,500 from both the USA and Britain.

The Nationalists gradually won territory in the north and south, taking Barcelona in January 1939, as the Republican cause fragmented through internal division. The ferocity of the war shocked the world, as Spanish civilians were slaughtered by German aerial bombardment and each side committed atrocities. On 28 March, the Nationalists marched into Madrid and General Franco ruled as a fascist dictator in Spain until his death in 1975.

UP TO 300,000 CIVILIANS MASSACRED

During the early years of the Sino-Japanese War (1937–45), Japan occupied large areas of eastern China. In December 1937, Japanese troops entered the Chinese capital of Nanjing and embarked upon uncontrolled murder, rape and looting. Within six weeks, between 60,000 and 300,000 Chinese civilians and POWs lost their lives and a third of the city's buildings were destroyed. Japanese forces were later diverted to fighting in the Pacific theatre and South-East Asia, the Allied defeat of Japan in 1945 ending its occupation of China. The massacre at Nanjing symbolized for many the barbarity and cruelty of the Japanese, a reputation that lasted throughout the war and beyond.

6 PANZER DIVISIONS

In the early hours of 1 September 1939, Hitler invaded Poland. He launched about 1.5 million troops, made up of 40-odd infantry divisions, 6 armoured panzer divisions with some 2,400 tanks, 4 motorized divisions and mobilized infantry (carried in trucks and personnel carriers) and 1,929 up-to-date aircraft. The Polish army numbered about 1 million men, but it had very few tanks, armoured personnel carriers or anti-tank or anti-aircraft guns, with just 750 armoured vehicles and 900 outdated planes.

Thus, when the Germans unleashed their blitzkrieg – 'lightning war', an assault by fast-moving tanks and other armoured vehicles to punch holes in the enemy line, followed by waves of motorized troops, all under powerful air cover – the attack proved unstoppable. Germany's well-trained panzer divisions were a force without equal in Europe (the Allies had lots of tanks but no armoured divisions in 1939).

Two days after Germany's invasion of Poland, Britain and France abandoned their former policies of appeasement and declared war on Germany. As a result of a secret Nazi-Soviet pact, Soviet forces entered Poland from the east on 17 September and in just a few days overran 77,000 square miles of territory, with just 4,000 Soviet casualties.

By 28 September, Poland was largely defeated, its resistance collapsing after Warsaw suffered two weeks of intensive bombing (around 30,000 shells a day). Poland was partitioned between Germany and the Soviet Union: around 1.5 million Poles, mostly civilians in the east, were captured by the Soviets, 350,000 losing their lives, with at least 25,000 Poles executed in Soviet prisons. The Germans took around 700,000 Polish prisoners. Seventy thousand Polish soldiers were killed and more than 130,000 injured. The Germans lost 16,000 troops and 30,000 were wounded.

ROLLS-ROYCE PV-12 ENGINE WITH 1,030 HORSEPOWER

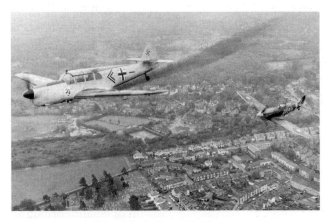

A German Messerschmitt with a Spitfire on its tail

After a six-month lull during which Hitler regrouped his forces, in April 1940 German panzer divisions continued their blitzkrieg invasion of Denmark and Norway, then Belgium, Holland and France. By 22 June, France had fallen, two weeks after the German advance in northern France had cut off Allied forces, leading to the evacuation of some 338,000 British and French troops from beaches at Dunkirk. Thereon, France was occupied by German troops with a collaborative government Vichy under Marshal Philippe Pétain.

Britain now stood alone as Germany launched a major bombing offensive in August 1940, targeting industrial centres, railways and the RAF's airfields. At the beginning of what became known as the Battle of Britain, the RAF had just 650 fighter aircraft to defend the country against the might of the German Luftwaffe, which had almost 800 fighters and over 1,000 bombers ready for operations, with hundreds more aircraft in reserve.

Britain's Fighter Command employed Hurricane planes to fight off bombers, and Supermarine Spitfires to combat Germany's fighter planes. With a Rolls-Royce PV-12 engine (later called a Merlin) of 1,030 horsepower, Spitfires gave exceptional performance at high altitude and were faster and just as manoeuvrable as their chief opponent the German Messerschmitt Bf 109. The Spitfire, many would argue, along with Britain's advanced radar warning system, gave the RAF the edge that it desperately needed, ensuring that the Luftwaffe failed to gain air superiority over southern Britain.

As a result, Hitler postponed, then later abandoned his planned invasion of Britain, switching almost entirely to night raids from September 1940. Sustained bombing of British cities until May 1941 (known as the 'Blitz') killed about 40,000 civilians.

1 in 5 British Fighter Pilots Killed

During the Battle of Britain, the RAF lost 544 fighter pilots – 1 in 5 – and 801 Bomber Command aircrew. The Luftwaffe lost 2,698 aircrew.

1,000 Allied Bombers in 1 Raid

On 15 May 1940, the RAF flew its first strategic bombing raid on Germany. From 1942, bombing raids increasingly targeted industrial sites and then civilian areas. Firebombing killed about 42,000 civilians in Hamburg in 1943, and some 80,000 civilians in Dresden in 1945 – a controversial measure to this day.

With the help of the United States, Allied raids on German cities involved as many as 1,000 bombers in a single raid. It has been estimated that Allied bombing killed around 400,000–600,000 civilians in Germany and around 67,000 in France. Around 60,000 British people died as a result of German bombing.

Invasion Force of 3.6 Million

On 22 June 1941, Germany launched the biggest and most powerful invasion force in history against its former ally, the Soviet Union. Axis forces consisted of 3.6 million troops with 3,600 tanks and 2,700 modern aircraft. The Soviets deployed 2.5 million troops, and approximately three times as many tanks and aircraft (10,000 tanks and 8,000 aircraft), though their planes were outdated compared with the German aircraft.

The ambitious operation, codenamed Operation Barbarossa, was driven by Hitler's ambition to rid himself of the Soviet threat and eradicate Bolshevism by building a German empire in the east. He also had eyes on the Soviet Union's vast supplies of raw materials and commodities, along with its oil reserves in the Caucasus. The Germans advanced in three groups along a 1,800-mile front, and by October 1941 they had surrounded Leningrad (today renamed St Petersburg), starting a 900-day siege, reached the outskirts of Moscow, and captured the Ukrainian capital of Kiev, taking 3 million Soviet prisoners in the process. In November, a German attack on Moscow led to a Soviet counter-attack that threw the Germans back some 200 miles in January 1942.

The German offensive to capture Stalingrad (now Volgograd) began in late summer 1942 and degenerated into building-to-building fighting. A Soviet Red Army counteroffensive in late November 1942 eventually led to the encirclement of two German armies. By late January 1943, General von Paulus, disobeying Hitler's orders to fight to the death, surrendered – 91,000 frozen and starving Germans were handed over to the Soviets, all but 5,000 or 6,000 of them later dying in Soviet prisons or labour camps. Total Axis casualties are believed to be 800,000 (killed, wounded or captured). Around 1.1 million Red Army soldiers were killed or wounded during the defence of Stalingrad, with 40,000 civilians also killed.

Hitler's failure to defeat the Soviet Union marked a major turning point in the war. The clash between the world's two largest armies inflicted appalling casualties. It is impossible to put a precise figure on the number of Soviets killed by the invasion, but estimates point to around 27 million, more than half of the fatalities being civilians. Many died during the fighting but millions, including Jews, Soviet officials and ordinary citizens, were executed by the Germans. Others died from famine or disease.

8 US Battleships Destroyed

On the morning of 7 December 1941, without warning, the Japanese launched a ferocious airborne attack on the US Pacific Fleet stationed at Pearl Harbor on the Hawaiian island of Oahu. In a couple of hours, eight US battleships were sunk or badly damaged and 2,400 US servicemen killed.

The attack provoked the US to join the war on the side of the Allies (British Prime Minister Winston Churchill claimed he slept 'the sleep of the saved' that night). Thereafter an American fleet, aided by breaking enemy codes, defeated the Japanese fleet at the Battle of the Coral Sea in May 1942 and the Battle of Midway the following month. By 1943, the US had effective air and sea dominance in the Pacific and recaptured several occupied Japanese territories.

20 Cigarettes a Day

US troops in the Pacific were supplied with twenty cigarettes a day during the Second World War. Each Italian trooper in North Africa carried his own personal espresso maker.

159 Million Million Million Settings

In 1932, the Polish secret service had managed to break into the Enigma, a complex cipher machine used by the Germans to communicate encoded information. By the outbreak of war, however, the Enigma's intricate system of wheels and three to five rotors was being reset by the Germans at least once a day, creating a possible 159 million million million new combination settings.

Nonetheless, in January 1940, mathematicians at Bletchley Park in Britain managed to break the Enigma system and decipher encoded messages. They were aided considerably by high-speed electro-mechanical devices known as Bombes, which ran through all the possible wheel configurations in order to detect the latest setting.

Intelligence passed on by the Enigma code-breakers, along with advances in radar, helped the British Admiralty to reroute ships away from German U-boat 'wolf packs' during the Battle of the Atlantic (in 1942, U-boat attacks on Allied merchant shipping sank an average of ninety-six ships a month). Enigma intelligence – codenamed 'Ultra' by the British – was also crucial in Allied victories in North Africa (enabling the Royal Navy to cut the German supply lines), in Italy and in the D-Day landings (see pages 178–9), helping to confuse Hitler over where the Allies were to land, the source of the invasion's success.

33,761 SHOT AT BABI YAR RAVINE

As Germany gained control of the Baltic States and western Soviet Union, mass shootings of Jewish civilians escalated to horrific proportions. In September 1941, all Jews in Kiev were ordered to appear at a point in the city so they could be resettled. Instead they were driven to the edge of the Babi Yar ravine and shot, each person ordered to lie down on the pile of mounting corpses before they themselves were gunned down. Within thirty-six hours, 33,761 people had been killed. Throughout the region (mainly the western Soviet states, eastern Poland, Lithuania, Latvia and Estonia) entire communities of men, women and children were killed in this manner, totalling around 1 million Jews by the end of 1941.

Mass shootings of civilians in German-occupied lands continued throughout 1942, with gas vans, as first tested on Soviet POWS, also utilized. Further west, the 'final solution' to the Jewish 'problem', as decided by Nazi leaders in 1942, came in the form of labour camps and death camps, six of which were built in Poland purely for the purposes of murder. The Reinhard death camps (named after Gestapo chief Reinhard Heydrich) killed around 1.5 million Jews, along with Soviet and Polish POWs, homosexuals, the disabled and mentally ill and other minority groups transported from across Nazi-occupied land. Of the Jewish population, approximately 6 million were killed by the German military.

1 Million Jews Killed At Auschwitz

In the Polish extermination camp at Auschwitz, 1 million Jews were murdered, beaten, starved and gassed by their Nazi captors. Other camps were the scenes of similar atrocities. At Treblinka 750,000 died; at Belzec 500,000; at Sobibor 200,000; at Kulmhof 150,000; at Lublin 50,000. There were many other camps where others whom the Nazis considered to be undesirable were put to death, but the Jews suffered most: up to 3 million died in the camps.

5 NORMANDY BEACHES

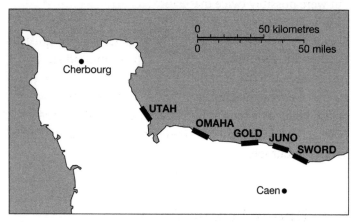

D-Day landing sites, 1944

By 1944, the German hold on Europe was weakening and the Allied invasion of Normandy (known as D-Day) was put into effect. On 6 June 1994, the Germans were caught off-guard as 156,000 Allied soldiers landed on five Normandy beaches: Utah, Omaha, Gold, Juno and Sword Beach. The largest seaborne invasion in history, the Allied armada consisted of 3,000 landing craft, 2,500 other ships and 500 naval vessels. The previous night, 822 aircraft had formed the vanguard of the invasion, dropping parachutists and towing gliders inland, with 13,000 aircraft supporting troops during the day.

The Allied troops landed under heavy fire from gun emplacements, British and Canadian troops landing on Gold, Juno and Sword beaches, and American forces on Utah and Omaha. The US First Division suffered the heaviest gunfire on Omaha at a cost of more than 2,000 casualties. Total Allied casualties on the first day were at least 10,000, with 4,414 confirmed dead. German casualties numbered at least 4,000, but were possibly twice that figure.

Allied forces eventually broke through the German defences, liberating Paris on 25 August. Thereafter, the Allies pushed through Europe, repulsing a German counter-attack in the Ardennes at the Battle of the Bulge. In March 1945, the Allies entered Germany and linked up with the Soviet Army. Staring at defeat, Hitler shot himself on 30 April, and on 8 May 1945, the Allies accepted Germany's unconditional surrender and declared Victory in Europe.

B-29 DROPS ATOMIC BOMB

In the Pacific theatre, the war continued. From March 1945, American bombers firebombed Tokyo and other Japanese cities, leading to the deaths of between 350,000 and 500,000 Japanese civilians. US forces stormed the Japanese islands of Iwo Jima and Okinawa by the end of June, but Japan refused to surrender.

As a consequence, on 6 August, a B-29 Superfortress bomber named *Enola Gay* dropped an atomic bomb, 'Little Boy', on the Japanese city of Hiroshima, immediately killing 80,000 people. Another B-29, *Bockscar*, dropped a second A-bomb, 'Fat Man', on Nagasaki three days later, killing around 40,000 people. Many others would later die from radiation poisoning and burns. This, combined with the Soviet Union's declaration of war on Japan on 14 August, led to the surrender of Japan.

OVER 50 MILLION LIVES LOST

The Second World War resulted in a death toll of over 50 million people, at least 35 million of whom were civilians (20 million from the Soviet Union and 5.7 million from Poland). Between 10 and 17 million civilians were deliberately exterminated as a result of Nazi ideological policies. Over 100 million people were under arms, the highest proportion of people in modern history.

51 FOUNDING MEMBERS OF THE UNITED NATIONS

The idea for the United Nations, its aim to ensure peace, security and cooperation among the world's nations, was initially articulated in 1941 by US President Franklin D. Roosevelt and Winston Churchill. The first United Nations meeting took place in San Francisco on 25 April 1945, attended by representatives from fifty countries around the world. Poland was not present but was permitted to become a founding member.

The United Nations charter was signed and promulgated on 24 October 1945. The Security Council's five permanent members, who have the power to veto any substantive resolution, were (and are today): France, China, the United Kingdom, the United States and the Russian Federation (in 1945 the Soviet Union). There are currently 193 member states in the United Nations.

FUTURE NUMBERS

The Second World War created a hugely significant historical watershed that changed the face of the world. We had taken the first steps into the nuclear age that would see an uneasy stand-off between the superpowers in the east and the west during the Cold War that would last for more than half a century. But new technologies and innovations given urgent impetus during the war brought invaluable benefits in peacetime, not least in the medical field with the widespread use of X-rays, antibiotics and immunization.

Despite periodic economic downturns, natural disasters and conflicts that continue to erupt around the globe, more people today live longer, live a healthier lifestyle and have a far higher standard of living than ever before, and the Second World War was the main catalyst that instigated changes in the modern age. If the pace of progress we have seen since the end of that landmark is maintained, then the numbers are looking good for the future.

BIBLIOGRAPHY

Brazier, Chris, *The No-Nonsense Guide to World History* (New Internationalist, 2001)

Bryson, Bill, *At Home* (Doubleday, 2010)

D'Efilippo, Valentina and Ball, James, *The Infographic History of the World* (HarperCollins, 2013)

Daniel, Clifton, *Chronicle of America* (Simon & Schuster, 1989)

Ferguson, Niall, *Civilization – The Six Killer Apps of Western Power* (Allen Lane, 2011)

Green, Rod, *Wonders of the Ancient World* (Templar)

Hastings, Max, *All Hell Let Loose – The World at War 1939–1945* (HarperCollins, 2011)

Haywood, John, *The Ancient World* (Quercus, 2010)

Hobbes, Nicholas, *Essential Militaria* (Atlantic Books, 2003)

MacGregor, Neil, *A History of the World in 100 Objects* (Allen Lane, 2010)

Marr, Andrew, *A History of the World* (Pan Macmillan, 2012)

Marriott, Emma, *Bad History – How We Got the Past Wrong* (Michael O'Mara, 2011)

Marriott, Emma, *The History of the World in Bite-Sized Chunks* (Michael O'Mara, 2012)

Martin, Guy, *How Britain Worked* (Virgin Books, 2012)

Martin, Guy, *Speed* (Virgin Books, 2014)

Oxford Children's History of the World (Oxford University Press, 2000)

Oxford Dictionary of World History (Oxford University Press, 2000)

Reynolds, David, *America – Empire of Liberty* (Allen Lane, 2009)

Roberts, J. M. *History of the World* (Helicon, 1976)

Rogerson, Barnaby, *Rogerson's Book of Numbers* (Profile Books, 2013)

Townson, Duncan, *The New Penguin Dictionary of Modern History 1789–1945* (Penguin Books, 1994)

Websites

www.archives.gov
www.bl.uk/world-war-one/articles/colonial-troops
www.britannica.com
www.freetheslaves.net
www.historytoday.com
www.irlandeses.org
www.loc.gov
www.nationalarchives.gov.uk
www.nationaltrust.org
www.ncpedia.org
www.pbs.org
www.physics.bu.edu
www.princeton.edu
www.scholastic.com
www.teara.govt.nz
www.telephonymuseum.com

Picture Acknowledgements

Bell Telephone (page 145): Courtesy of the Library of Congress, LC-USZ62-117582

Boston Tea Party (page 114): Courtesy of the Library of Congress, LC-DIG-ds-03379

Colonial Africa (page 148): Map by David Woodroffe

Columns (page 37): Shutterstock

Crusader (page 66): Clipart.com

Cuneiform (page 21): Shutterstock

Easter Island Head (page 55): Shutterstock

Fertile Crescent (page 11): Map by David Woodroffe

Gandhi (page 165): Popperfoto / Getty Images

Gutenberg Bible (page 80): Illustration from *Printing: Its Birth and Growth* by William Jaggard, 1908

Heinz (page 143): The Literary Digest, 1910

Knossos (page 23): De Agostini Picture Library / Getty Images

Louisiana Purchase (page 127): Map by David Woodroffe

Mandela (page 150): AFP / Getty Images

Model T Ford (page 163): Courtesy of the Library of Congress, LC-USZ62-21222

Napoleon (page 124): Clipart.com

Nazi Rally (page 167) Illustrated London News

Normandy Beaches (page 178): Map by David Woodroffe

Oceanic Exploration (page 88): Map by David Woodroffe

Pieces of Eight (page 90): iStock

Quipu (page 77): Illustration by David Woodroffe

Seven Wonders (page 18–20): Illustration of the Pyramids from The Seven Wonders of the World by Theodore Buckley, 1854; engraving of the Hanging Gardens of Babylon, unknown, 19th century; engravings of the Temple of Artemis, Statue of Zeus, Mausoleum at Halicarnassus, Colossus of Rhodes, Lighthouse of Alexandria by Philip Galle after Maarten van Heemskerck

Peacock Throne (page 112) : Clipart.com
Roskilde Ship (page 62): Illustration by David Woodroffe
Silk Road (page 42): Map by David Woodroffe
Spanish Armada Routes (page 92): Map by David Woodroffe
Spitfire/Messerschmitt (page 171): Press Association Images
Terracotta Warriors (page 39): Shutterstock
Tughra (page 85): Illustration by David Woodroffe
Viceroy Tulip (page 100): Illustration by David Woodroffe
Vitruvian Man (page 82): Shutterstock

INDEX

A

Abbas I, Shah 95
Abbasid caliphate 53
abolition of slavery 140–1
aboriginal population, Australia 123, 152
Achaemenes of Persia, King 29
Acre, Israel 67
Act of Supremacy (1534) 84
African colonies, European 147–50, 158
African National Congress (ANC) 150
Agincourt (1415), Battle of 72
agricultural revolution, Britain 119–20
Aksum Empire, Africa 50
Alexander the Great 24, 33, 35–6
Alexandria, Egypt 20, 35–6
algebra 53, 66
American Civil War 138, 139–40, 141
American Telephone & Telegraph 146
Americas *see* Mexico; New Spain; New World;
    North America; Peru; Spanish America
Amorites 12
Amritsar Massacre (1919) 165
Anatolia 22
animal domestication 11
Anyang 25
apartheid system 150
Archaic Period, Greek 32, 33
Archimedes 36
Argentina 129
Artemis, temple of 19
Artemisia II of Caria 19
Arthur, King 54
Artistotle 31, 33, 35
Aryabhata 48
Ashanti Empire, Africa 108, 147
Ashoka, Emperor 38
Ashurbanipal of Assyria, King 26
Askia Dynasty (Songhai Empire) 75
Assyrians 26
astronomy 25–6, 57–8
Atahualpa 89
Athens 31, 32, 34
atomic bombs 179
Attila the Hun 48
Augustus, Emperor 43, 44
Aurangzeb, Mughal Emperor 104–5
Auschwitz death camp, Poland 177
Austerlitz (1805), Battle of 124
Australia 90–1, 122–3, 157–8
Australian aboriginal population 123

Austria 110, 124, 126, 131, 132, 153
Austrian Succession, War of the 110
Austro-Prussian War 132
automobile industry 162–3
Avenue of the Dead, Teotihuacan 59
Aztecs 78–9, 89

B

Babylonians 17, 18, 25–6, 29, 51
Baghdad 53
banknotes, first 65, 139
Barbarossa, Frederick 67
Battle of Britain 172–3
Battle of the Atlantic 176
Battle of the Bulge 179
Bede 51
Bedford, Duke of 72
Belgium 125, 126, 129, 131, 155
Bell, Alexander Graham 145–6
Bible 44–5, 80–1, 83
Bill of Rights (1689) 105
Bismarck, Otto von 132
Black Death 68, 72–3
the Blitz 172
Boer War 149
Bohemia 97
Boleyn, Anne 84
Bolívar, Simón 128–9
Bolsheviks 160, 167, 174
Borodino (1812), Battle of 124
Boston Tea Party 114–15
Boudicca, Queen 46
Boxer Rebellion 151
Boyaca (1819), Battle of 128
Brazil 108, 129, 141
Britain 46, 47, 54, 56, 57, 61, 63–4, 101–2, 108,
    115–16, 119–21, 124, 125, 126, 128, 129, 134,
    136–7, 145, 147, 149, 150, 154, 156, 157–8, 161,
    164, 165, 170, 172–3, 176, 178–9, 180
    see also England; Ireland; Scotland
British War Office 156
Buddha (Siddhartha Gautama) 37–8, 61
Byzantine Empire 49, 73

C

Cairo, Egypt 74
calendars 33, 51, 52, 57, 119
Calvin, John 83